365
SUCCESSFUL DAYS

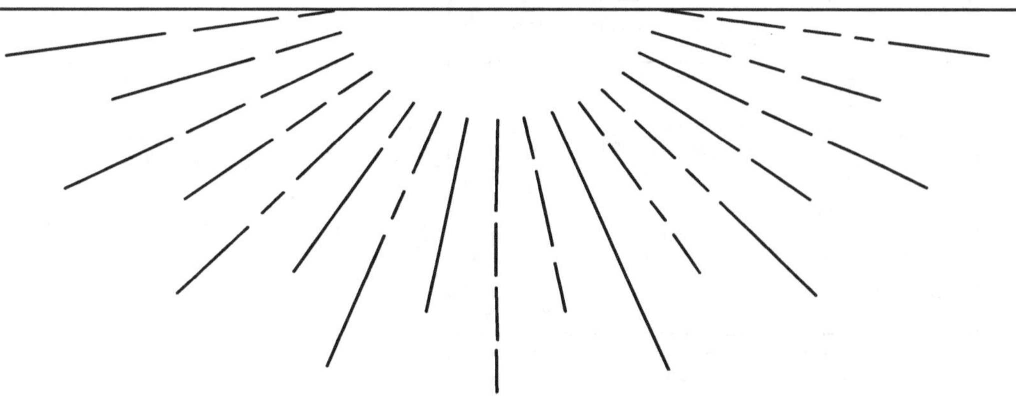

GET TO KNOW OUR BOOKS
BY ACCESSING HERE!

First edition in 2023

Chair: Paulo Roberto Houch
MTB 0083982/SP

Author: Paola Houch
Art Coordination: Rubens Martim
Design: Gabrielle Cardoso
Sales Phone: +55 (11) 3393-7727 (comercial2@editoraonline.com.br)

Legal depository was made.

Dados Internacionais de Catalogação na Publicação (CIP) de acordo com ISBD	
H835t	Houch, Paola
	365 Successful Days / Paola Houch. Barueri, SP : Camelot Editora, 2023.
	128 p. ; 15,1cm x 23cm.
	ISBN: 978-65-6095-030-6
	1. Autoajuda. I. Título.
2023-3606	CDD 158.1 CDU 159.97
Elaborado por Vagner Rodolfo da Silva - CRB-8/9410	

All rights reserved to
IBC – Instituto Brasileiro de Cultura LTDA
CNPJ 04.207.648/0001-94
Avenida Juruá, 762 – Alphaville Industrial
CEP. 06455-010 – Barueri/SP
www.editoraonline.com.br

365 SUCCESSFUL DAYS

SUMMARY

INTRODUCTION

Every day is unique, and each day you have new opportunities for greatness. Today is your canvas, and you hold the paintbrush to create a masterpiece of success and fulfillment.

Keep in mind that success is a journey marked by development, resilience, and determination, so embrace each day with a strong desire to be the best version of yourself. Staying motivated every day and maintaining focus on your personal goals are the keys that unlock the door to success and fulfillment.

The route of life is full of detours, turns, and unforeseen difficulties. Along the road, it's normal to experience times of uncertainty, exhaustion, or distraction, but it's precisely at these times that the value of maintaining concentration becomes clear. Embrace the process, and trust that every experience is shaping you for greatness. Believe in your abilities, for you possess the power to create your reality. You are destined for greatness.

Celebrate every achievement, no matter how small, acknowledge your progress, and take pride in each step you take toward your goals. Every effort counts, and every moment of dedication brings you closer to the success you deserve. Visualize your success and hold that image in your mind. See yourself achieving your dreams, living the life you desire, and making a positive impact on the world. Your mind is a powerful tool, so program it for success.

Today is the day to take charge of your destiny. Let motivation be your constant companion, driving you forward to create the life you envision. Success is not a distant dream; it's within your reach, waiting for you to seize it.

You have the power to make it happen. Embrace the journey, stay persistent, and believe in yourself. Success is not just an end goal; it's a state of mind. Embrace the mindset of a champion, and you will undoubtedly achieve greatness.

Go forth and conquer, for your time is now.

As you embark on this literary journey, may the ideas within these pages inspire you.

Paola Houch

January 1st

"Success is not final, failure is not fatal: It is the courage to continue that counts." – Winston Churchill

Success should never lead to complacency, as there are always new heights to reach and challenges to conquer. Similarly, failure should not discourage us from pursuing our goals; instead, it offers invaluable lessons for growth and improvement.

January 2nd

"The only limit to our realization of tomorrow will be our doubts of today." – Franklin D. Roosevelt

Our doubts and fears can be the biggest hurdles in achieving our dreams and aspirations. Often, it is not external factors but our internal struggles that hold us back from reaching our full potential.

By recognizing and challenging these doubts, we can break free from their grip and open up a world of possibilities. Believing in ourselves and our abilities is crucial. When we trust in our capabilities and cultivate a positive mindset, we unlock the door to untapped potential and greatness.

January 3rd

"Happiness is not something ready-made. It comes from your own actions." – Dalai Lama

By taking responsibility for our actions, attitudes, and outlook on life, we can shape our happiness from within. It involves cultivating positive habits, practicing gratitude, fostering meaningful relationships, and pursuing activities that bring us joy. Embracing a positive mindset and taking proactive steps towards our goals can lead us on a path of contentment and fulfillment.

January 4th

*"The only thing standing between you and your goal is the story
you keep telling yourself as to why you can't achieve it."*
— Jordan Belfort

Our thoughts have a tremendous influence on our actions and behaviors. When we continually tell ourselves negative stories, doubts, or excuses, we inadvertently sabotage our progress. These self-imposed limitations become barriers that impede our growth and potential. However, recognizing this truth empowers us to take control of our narrative and rewrite the story. By challenging those limiting beliefs and reframing our thoughts, we can build a new narrative that fosters determination, self-belief, and resilience.

January 5th

"In the middle of difficulty lies opportunity." — Albert Einstein

Amidst difficulties and obstacles, there are opportunities waiting to be discovered and harnessed. Life is filled with ups and downs, and it's during the tough times when we often feel the most tested and vulnerable. However, it is precisely in these moments of struggle that we have the chance to grow, learn, and find new paths forward.

January 6th

"The future belongs to those who believe in the beauty of their dreams."
– Eleanor Roosevelt

Belief acts as the driving force that propels us forward. When we have unwavering faith in our dreams, we are more likely to take bold actions, make courageous decisions, and persist through adversity. It's important to remember that believing in our dreams doesn't guarantee a smooth path or immediate success, but it does give us the strength to endure and navigate the challenges along the way.

January 7th

"I know of no better life purpose than to perish in attempting the great and the impossible." – Friedrich Wilhelm Nietzsche

The human spirit has been uplifted throughout history by those who dared to dream big, challenge the status quo, and reach for the stars. It is the individuals who fearlessly pursue audacious goals and ideas that have often made the greatest impact on the world.

January 8th

"Believe you can and you're halfway there." – Theodore Roosevelt

The first step towards success is having faith in ourselves and our abilities. Belief in ourselves creates a self-fulfilling prophecy. When we have confidence in our capabilities, we tend to make better decisions, work harder, and attract opportunities that align with our aspirations.

January 9th

"Don't be afraid to give up the good to go for the great."
– John D. Rockefeller

Choosing greatness over the good may be intimidating, as it involves uncertainty and the possibility of failure. Making the decision to give up what is good requires courage and a clear vision of what we want to achieve, but by being fearless in our pursuit of greatness, we open ourselves up to new possibilities and a more fulfilling life. So, let's not settle for mediocrity when greatness awaits us.

January 10th

"Your time is limited, don't waste it living someone else's life. Don't be trapped by dogma – which is living with the results of other people's thinking." – Steve Jobs

Time is indeed limited, and each passing moment is an opportunity that can never be reclaimed. Breaking free from the expectations of others allows us to stay true to ourselves, to fully live and enjoy our own lives. Let's cherish the limited time we have, and instead of following the crowd, let's dare to be ourselves unapologetically.

January 11th

"Success is not about the destination; it's about the journey." – Zig Ziglar

Success is not merely a final endpoint but rather a series of experiences, growth, and learning that occur along the way. We must savor the small victories, celebrate progress, and find joy in the process of working towards our goals. This teaches us to appreciate the present moment and not solely focus on the end result.

January 12th

"The best way to predict the future is to create it." – Peter Drucker

Instead of passively waiting for the future to unfold, we hold the power to influence the outcomes by our actions and choices. The mindset of actively creating the future cultivates a sense of ownership and responsibility. The power to shape our lives lies within us.

January 13th

"Success is walking from failure to failure with no loss of enthusiasm."
– Winston Churchill

This quote is a powerful testament to the resilience and perseverance required to achieve success. It conveys the idea that success is not an easy or straightforward path; instead, it often involves encountering failures and setbacks along the way. Embracing failures as learning experiences, rather than viewing them as defeats, is what separates those who succeed from those who give up.

January 14th

"What you get by achieving your goals is not as important as what you become by achieving your goals." – Zig Ziglar

While achieving our goals is undoubtedly gratifying and can bring external recognition and material gains, it is the internal changes and character development that truly shape us as individuals. The process of working towards our goals challenges us to push beyond our comfort zones, confront our fears, and develop new skills. We develop a greater sense of self-awareness and self-confidence, allowing us to tackle future challenges with a newfound sense of empowerment.

January 15th

"Hardships often prepare ordinary people for an extraordinary destiny."
– C.S. Lewis

When we encounter difficulties, we are compelled to tap into our inner strength, courage, and determination. Overcoming hardships can shape our character and build resilience. So we must not be discouraged by hardships, but rather, embrace them as transformative opportunities. For it is through facing challenges that ordinary people can uncover their extraordinary destiny.

January 16th

"You miss 100% of the shots you don't take." – Wayne Gretzky

If we don't even try, we'll never achieve anything. Every successful individual or accomplishment began with someone taking a chance and daring to try. So, let's be brave and take those shots in life. It's only by taking action that we open doors to new possibilities and create a life filled with purpose and fulfillment.

January 17th

"The only person you are destined to become is the person you decide to be." – Ralph Waldo Emerson

Destiny is not some preordained, fixed fate that we have no control over. Instead, it is the culmination of our decisions, actions, and attitudes. By making conscious choices and taking responsibility for our lives, we have the ability to craft our own future.

January 18th

"The best revenge is massive success." – Frank Sinatra

Rather than being consumed by negative emotions or seeking retribution, striving for success allows us to rise above the negativity and focus on our own development. It enables us to transcend the situation and transform our pain into the fuel that propels us towards greatness. Choosing to seek success as a form of revenge promotes a healthier and more positive mindset. It fosters personal growth and allows us to direct our focus towards building a better future for ourselves rather than dwelling on the past.

January 19th

"Either you run the day, or the day runs you." – Jim Rohn

When we "run the day," we take charge of our schedules, prioritize our tasks, and make intentional decisions about how we want to spend our time. By doing so, we are better able to focus on our goals, stay productive, and make progress towards our aspirations. On the other hand, if we allow "the day to run us," we become reactive, letting external circumstances dictate our actions. This can lead to feelings of overwhelm, stress, and a sense of losing control over our lives.

January 20th

"You have within you right now, everything you need to deal with whatever the world can throw at you." – Brian Tracy

We possess the inner strength, abilities, and resources needed to tackle adversity. This reminds us of the importance of self-reliance and the power of taking responsibility for our actions and choices. By recognizing that we possess everything we need within ourselves, we become more empowered and less dependent on external factors.

January 21st

"The journey of a thousand miles begins with one step." – Lao Tzu

Even the most daunting and ambitious journeys must start with a single, courageous step. Each great accomplishment, no matter how grand, begins with a small action. So, let's not be discouraged by the distance that lies ahead. With the courage to take that first step and the determination to keep moving forward, we can achieve greatness.

January 22nd

"The greatest glory in living lies not in never falling, but in rising every time we fall." – Nelson Mandela

In life, falling or facing failure is inevitable. We all experience moments of disappointment, mistakes, and obstacles. Rather than being discouraged or disheartened by our falls, this quote encourages us to see them as opportunities for growth and learning. Each time we rise after falling, we become stronger, wiser, and more capable of handling future trials.

January 23rd

"Believe you can and you're halfway there." – Theodore Roosevelt

Having confidence in our abilities and believing in ourselves is a crucial step towards success. Our mindset has a significant influence on our actions and outcomes. When we genuinely believe in our capacity to achieve something, we are more likely to take initiative, stay committed, and overcome obstacles with determination.

January 24th

"The greater the obstacle, the more glory in overcoming it."
– Molière

The magnitude of the obstacle is directly proportional to the glory and pride we feel when we overcome it. Do not be afraid of facing great challenges, it often leads to the most glorious and rewarding moments.

January 25th

"Your belief determines your action and your action determines your results, but first, you have to believe." – Mark Victor Hansen

Belief acts as a powerful driving force that influences the way we approach challenges, pursue goals, and navigate through life. When we have strong, positive beliefs in our abilities and the possibility of success, we are more likely to take decisive and proactive actions.

January 26th

"The way to develop self-confidence is to do the thing you fear and get a record of successful experiences behind you."
– William Jennings Bryan

By taking action despite our apprehensions, we gradually diminish the power fear holds over us. Each time we confront our fears and succeed, we create a positive feedback loop. The memory of our past achievements reinforces our belief in our abilities, strengthening our self-confidence. As we accumulate a track record of successful experiences, our confidence continues to grow.

January 27th

"Life doesn't get easier or more forgiving, we get stronger and more resilient." – Steve Maraboli

Life is full of ups and downs, obstacles, and uncertainties. No matter how much we wish for an easier path, it is through facing these challenges that we learn, evolve, and become better versions of ourselves. Instead of waiting for an easier life, let's focus on becoming stronger and more resilient individuals.

January 28th

"When I let go of what I am, I become what I might be"- Laozi

Often, we hold onto identities, beliefs, or behaviors that no longer serve us. We may fear letting go of familiar aspects of ourselves because it feels safe and comfortable. However, this clinging can hinder personal growth and limit our possibilities for the future. When we shed our old skin and embrace the uncertainty of transformation, we become receptive to growth and development.

January 29th

"Those who are wise won't be busy, and those who are too busy can't be wise."– Lin Yutang, The Importance of Living

In today's fastpaced world, it's easy to get caught up in the hustle and bustle of everyday life, filling our schedules with endless tasks and commitments. However, this constant busyness can prevent us from taking the time to reflect, introspect, and gain valuable insights. On the other hand, those who prioritize wisdom understand the importance of creating space in their lives for meaningful pursuits, learning, and self-improvement.

January 30th

"When you believe in yourself, you have the first secret of success." – Norman Vincent Peale

Lack of self-belief can hold us back from reaching our full potential. If we don't believe we can succeed, we may never take the necessary actions to pursue our goals. It's essential to recognize that self-belief doesn't mean we will never experience moments of self-doubt or setbacks. However, having a strong foundation of belief in ourselves allows us to bounce back, learn from failures, and keep moving forward.

January 31st

"If you want to fly, you have to give up the things that weigh you down." – Toni Morrison

To truly soar and experience the freedom of flight, we must release the things that weigh us down. This may involve letting go of toxic relationships, negative thought patterns, self-limiting beliefs, or unfulfilling habits. Letting go can be challenging, as it often requires us to confront uncomfortable truths and step outside our comfort zones. However, it is through this process of release that we find liberation and open ourselves to new opportunities and possibilities.

February 1st

"Start each day with a positive thought and a grateful heart." – Roy T. Bennett, The Light in the Heart

A simple way to practice gratitude is to reflect on the people, experiences, and opportunities we are grateful for. Although life can be challenging at times, it is still full of blessings and choosing our attitude each day is within our power. It is important to choose positivity and gratitude consciously because we can have a positive impact on the lives of others and our overall well-being when we do so.

February 2nd

"The only constant in life is change." – Heraclitus

We live in a dynamic world full of transitions, transformations, and fluctuations. Our circumstances, relationships, careers, and even ourselves change over time. As we accept the fact that change is constant, we are able to think more creatively and adapt more quickly.

February 3rd

"Your work is going to fill a large part of your life, and the only way to be truly satisfied is to do what you believe is great work. And the only way to do great work is to love what you do." – Steve Jobs

A significant portion of our lives revolve around our work. Our overall happiness and well-being can be influenced by it. Therefore, it is vital that we find meaning and satisfaction in what we do.

Doing "great work" doesn't necessarily mean accomplishing notoriety or acknowledgment. Instead, it refers to the fulfillment that comes from contributing our unique skills and talents to something that we believe in.

February 4th

"Waste no more time arguing about what a good man should be. Be one." – Marcus Aurelius

Talking or speculating about being a nice person is insufficient. Living out those beliefs in our daily lives is what leads to real transformation and growth. Instead of wasting time debating, let's commit ourselves to living up to the values we cherish.

February 5th

"The only place where success comes before work is in the dictionary."
– Vidal Sassoon

Success cannot be accomplished without putting in the necessary time and effort. There are no shortcuts. Consistent work, tenacity, and the willingness to stretch ourselves beyond our comfort zones are the keys to success. Setting objectives, taking practical steps, and overcoming obstacles are all necessary.

February 6th

"To be yourself in a world that is constantly trying to make you something else is the greatest accomplishment." – Ralph Waldo Emerson

Being authentic to ourselves implies accepting all of our strengths, weaknesses, quirks, and imperfections. Honoring our values, interests, and views means doing so even when they may not be in line with what society expects of us. We develop a sense of self-worth and inner tranquility when we stay loyal to ourselves.

February 7th

"Not how long, but how well you have lived is the main thing."
– Seneca

The quote urges us to change our focus from an obsession with longevity to one that emphasizes the magnitude and richness of our experiences. It highlights the importance of loving others, being kind, compassionate, and growing personally. The quote also serves as a reminder that life isn't infinite and that we are all unaware of how much time we have left. This insight emphasizes how crucial it is to live in the present and avoid taking anything for granted.

February 8th

"Lack of direction, not lack of time, is the problem. We all have twenty-four hour days." – Zig Ziglar

Time can quickly pass us by if we don't have a clear plan and purpose, leaving us feeling unproductive and unfulfilled. Our time becomes more meaningful and purpose-driven when we have a sense of direction as it gives us a road map for our decisions and actions. Making a clear list of our objectives and goals enables us to efficiently manage our time and energy. It helps us to maintain our attention on the things that are most important while preventing distractions from derailing us from our path.

February 9th

"A goal without a plan is just a wish." – Antoine de Saint-Exupéry

Goals are the aspirations we have for the things we wish to achieve in life. They provide us focus, inspiration, and a sense of meaning. Goals, however, do not become attainable objectives without a clear plan of action.

February 10th

"Life is like riding a bicycle. To keep your balance, you must keep moving." – Albert Einstein

We face the risk of losing our sense of balance and becoming stagnant when we stop moving or fight change. It gets harder and harder to maintain stability, like trying to balance on a stationary bike. However, when we keep moving, we develop strength and endurance. No matter how modest, every step forward advances our development. We just have to keep going.

February 11th

"Life is really simple, but men insist on making it complicated."
– Confucius

Humans frequently overthink, overanalyze, and complicate situations beyond what is necessary. The quote encourages us to take a step back, declutter our lives, and concentrate on what is most important. It serves as a reminder that embracing simplicity and valuing the beauty of life's basic elements can frequently lead to pleasure and contentment.

February 12th

"The only true wisdom is in knowing you know nothing." – Socrates

Realizing the limits of our understanding is the first step on the path to wisdom. We are more open to learning from others and seeking knowledge from them when we recognize the extent to which we know. Accepting the notion that we don't know everything does not imply that we should be insecure or give up on our goals. Instead, it motivates us to approach life with a sense of curiosity, to ask questions, and to be open to lifelong learning.

February 13th

"Health is the greatest gift, contentment the greatest wealth, faithfulness the best relationship." – Buddha

We foster a more balanced and successful existence by putting health, contentment, and faithfulness first. These principles improve our interpersonal interactions and general well-being. The quote serves as a helpful reminder of the value of appreciating life's small pleasures. It encourages us to pay attention to what matters most and develop an emotion of gratitude for our blessings.

February 14th

"Opportunities multiply as they are seized." – Sun Tzu

The more we seize opportunities, the more they present themselves. When we take advantage of opportunities, we start a chain reaction that opens up additional doors and possibilities. By taking action, you can access fresh possibilities through making connections and learning new things. Of course, not every opportunity will bring immediate success, and some can even result in setbacks. Still, every experience teaches us something valuable and advances our personal and professional growth.

February 15th

"I believe every human has a finite number of heartbeats. I don't intend to waste any of mine." – Neil Armstrong

Different people may have different definitions of time waste. For some, it might be putting off completing crucial tasks, lingering on their previous errors, or becoming preoccupied with unimportant issues. For others it may be living without a purpose, ignoring their health, or skipping out on significant relationships. The quote advises us to be mindful in how we spend our time and energy. It pushes us to give priority to the things that make us happy, content, and have a sense of purpose.

February 16th

"Mostly it is loss which teaches us about the worth of things."
– Arthur Schopenhauer, Parerga and Paralipomena

While loss can be incredibly painful, it can also be a catalyst for personal growth and transformation. We can develop, change, and find resilience and significance in the face of hardship through the experience of loss.

February 17th

"The whole secret of a successful life is to find out what is one's destiny to do, and then do it."– Henry Ford

Understanding our passions, values, and talents on a deep level is necessary for the introspective journey that is finding our purpose. We find the way to personal fulfillment when we discover what truly touches our hearts and lights our inner fire.

February 18th

"Live as if you were to die tomorrow. Learn as if you were to live forever." – Mahatma Gandhi

The phrase "live as if you were to die tomorrow" encourages us to live urgently and to recognize the fleeting nature of life. Time is limited and valuable, so we must make the most of each day. The phrase "learn as if you were to live forever" highlights the need for lifelong learning and personal development. It encourages us to have an open, curious mind that is constantly searching out information and wisdom.

February 19th

"It had long since come to my attention that people of accomplishment rarely sat back and let things happen to them. They went out and happened to things." – Leonardo Da Vinci

Success doesn't happen without work and commitment. Achievers aren't afraid of perseverance and hard work; they know that working toward their objectives may require overcoming challenges and disappointments. Successful people take command of their lives and actively seek their goals and desires rather than waiting for opportunities to present themselves.

February 20th

"If you live long enough, you'll make mistakes. But if you learn from them, you'll be a better person." – Bill Clinton

We can learn and grow by owning up to our mistakes and accepting responsibility for them. They give us information about our flaws, blind spots, and opportunities to improve our knowledge and abilities. We may improve ourselves and pave the way to a more rewarding and richer life journey by taking the time to learn from our failures.

February 21st

"I can't change the direction of the wind, but I can adjust my sails to always reach my destination." – Jimmy Dean

While we may not have any influence over the outside world, we do have control over how we react to it and how we view it. The unpredictability and uncontrollable features of life are represented by the metaphor of the wind shifting direction. There will always be situations that we can't change, but what we can control is how we deal with those situations.

February 22nd

"If you're not stubborn, you'll give up on experiments too soon. And if you're not flexible, you'll pound your head against the wall and you won't see a different solution to a problem you're trying to solve." – Jeff Bezos

Stubbornness mixed with flexibility produces a dynamic attitude that encourages creativity, resilience, and lifelong learning. It enables us to be persistent in following our goal while remaining open to criticism, fresh suggestions, and chances for development.

February 23rd

"It takes 20 years to build a reputation and five minutes to ruin it. If you think about that, you'll do things differently." – Warren Buffett

The quote's underlying message advises us to exercise caution in our actions and choices by taking reputational impact into account. When we consider the value of reputation, we are more inclined to act honorably, choose wisely, and give long-term trust a higher priority than immediate benefits.

February 24th

"Be kind, for everyone you meet is fighting a hard battle." – Socrates

It is easy to forget that everyone around us is battling their own personal struggles. This quote challenges us to consider people's complex lives and feelings. A simple act of kindness, a warm smile, or a considerate gesture can make someone's day and give them hope while they are going through a tough period.

February 25th

"You must not lose faith in humanity. Humanity is an ocean; if a few drops of the ocean are dirty, the ocean does not become dirty."
– Mahatma Gandhi

The innumerable acts of generosity, compassion, and love that take place every day all across the world should not be overshadowed by the negativity or flaws of a small number of people. Humanity is as big and diverse as the ocean. Even in the face of unfavorable actions or behaviors from a few people, we must continue to have faith in the goodness of humanity.

February 26th

"Happiness is the feeling that power increases – that resistance is being overcome." – Friedrich Nietzsche

Happiness comes from a deeper sense of fulfillment that comes from conquering obstacles and going through personal development. When we trust that we have the power to overcome challenges and barriers in our lives, we experience true happiness.

February 27th

"You choose the life you live. If you don't like it, it's on you to change it because no one else is going to do it for you." – Kim Kiyosaki

We are the architects of our own destinies and have the ability to make decisions that will shape our future. The direction we take and the results we encounter are influenced by the decisions we make, both large and minor. It is not productive to wait for other people to improve our situation. We have the ability and obligation to bring about change if we are unhappy with any element of our existence.

February 28th

"If life were predictable it would cease to be life, and be without flavor."
– Eleanor Roosevelt

Life's unpredictable nature is its fundamental essence, and embracing the unexpected makes life richer and more exciting. While seeking consistency and predictability is natural, it's equally important to understand that life's surprises give our existence meaning and purpose.

March 1st

"Be content with what you have; rejoice in the way things are. When you realize there is nothing lacking, the whole world belongs to you." – Lao Tzu

The principles of mindfulness and intentional living are supported by this quote. It encourages us to slow down, be present, and find joy in the richness of the now. By accepting that there is nothing lacking, we free ourselves from the constant need for approval from others, which enables us to have deeper relationships with both ourselves and the world around us.

March 2nd

"If I cannot do great things, I can do small things in a great way."
– Martin Luther King Jr.

In a society where success is frequently determined by significant achievements, greatness can be discovered in the everyday moments of life. We can have a lasting effect and advance society by putting passion, dedication, and integrity into even the simplest deeds.

March 3rd

"It's not the years in your life that count. It's the life in your years."
– Abraham Lincoln

This quote motivates us to consider our time management and how we can make the most of each priceless moment. It encourages us to set aside the insignificant and embrace what's important. Our years become more vibrant and meaningful when we concentrate on the life we bring into them.

March 4th

"Being deeply loved by someone gives you strength, while loving someone deeply gives you courage." – Lao Tzu

When we are surrounded by love, whether from a partner, family, or friends, we acquire a greater resilience. It's as if love wraps us in a protective shield, giving us the strength to face even the most difficult challenges with grace and perseverance. Let us embrace love in all of its forms – as a source of joy, a catalyst for growth, and a powerful force that enables us to navigate life's journey with unfailing strength and resilience.

March 5th

"It does not do to dwell on dreams and forget to live." – J.K. Rowling

Humans have a tendency to lose themselves in daydreams, make constant plans for the future, or dwell on the past. By keeping our feet grounded in the present, we develop mindfulness and a love for the transitory moments that make up our existence. Let us not neglect the richness of the current experience in the pursuit of our dreams.

March 6th

"It is not enough to have a good mind; the main thing is to use it well."
– Rene Descartes

Intelligence by itself cannot ensure happiness or success; rather, what matters most is how we decide to apply it. Let's keep in mind that how well we use our knowledge rather than simply how much we know is the actual test of our intelligence as we go through life.

March 7th

"People are like dirt. They can either nourish you and help you grow as a person or they can stunt your growth and make you wilt and die." – Plato

Our perspective, convictions, and values can be influenced by the individuals we spend time with. Their impact can be extremely important in assisting us in becoming the best versions of ourselves. We can design a life that promotes development, resiliency, and wellbeing by fostering positive relationships and being aware of toxic influences.

March 8th

"My heart is at ease knowing that what was meant for me will never miss me, and that what misses me was never meant for me." – Al-Shafi'i

While we can work hard to achieve our objectives and pursue our dreams, we must also have faith in the process and be prepared for any surprising turns life may take. The biggest blessings often come from unexpected detours.

March 9th

"Cry. Forgive. Learn. Move on. Let your tears water the seeds of your future happiness." – Steve Maraboli

When we accept our feelings, draw lessons from our past, and make the decision to go forward with courage and optimism, we may heal and grow. Let yourself grieve, be forgiving, and take lessons from your mistakes. Instead of concentrating on the past, let it serve as a starting point for development and the foundation for future happiness.

March 10th

"When you cease to dream you cease to live." – Malcolm Forbes

Dreams are not just wishes; they are also visions of what may be. We bring excitement, passion, and a feeling of purpose into our lives by cultivating and pursuing our dreams. By doing this, we liberate life's potential and set off on a journey that will truly make it remarkable.

March 11th

"Every moment is a fresh beginning." – T.S. Eliot

We have the ability to influence our future and make the most of each fresh moment, regardless of what happened in the past. Accept the excitement of each beginning and let go of whatever restrictions you may have placed on yourself. We may live truthfully and make the most of the priceless gift that life gives us each day by accepting the possibilities of new beginnings.

March 12th

"We are what we repeatedly do. Excellence, then, is not an act but a habit." – Aristotle

Excellence is a reflection of the decisions we make every day, not a one-time event. When we consistently engage in activities that are in accordance with excellence, they embed themselves in our character and produce amazing results. Making excellence a habit helps us build a solid foundation for success and fulfillment over the long term.

March 13th

"You never change your life until you step out of your comfort zone; change begins at the end of your comfort zone." – Roy T. Bennett

Our comfort zone may be restricting and keep us from reaching our greatest potential. We discover hidden qualities and talents that may have been dormant by taking risks and exploring the unknown. We need to be willing to go beyond what is comfortable and familiar if we are to make meaningful change in our lives.

March 14th

"Have more than you show, speak less than you know."
– William Shakespeare, King Lear

One should not brag or flaunt their accomplishments or assets. By embracing humility, we may stay grounded and steer clear of arrogance. The quote emphasizes how important content is in comparison to superficiality. It is more crucial to concentrate on laying a solid foundation of knowledge and character than it is to look for approval from others.

March 15th

"The greatest weapon against stress is our ability to choose one thought over another." – William James

Being conscious of our thoughts and how they affect our emotions is crucial for stress management. Instead of letting stress overwhelm us, we can decide to respond to it in a way that strengthens us. We must recognize harmful thought patterns and consciously decide to change the focus to more uplifting and positive thoughts.

March 16th

"You may not control all the events that happen to you, but you can decide not to be reduced by them." – Maya Angelou

Keep in mind that how we respond to the events in life can influence how they affect us. By making the decision to not let difficulties define us, we embrace the power we already possess to face problems head-on and come out stronger and more resilient.

March 17th

"Incredible change happens in your life when you decide to take control of what you do have power over instead of craving control over what you don't." – Steve Maraboli, Life, the Truth, and Being Free

We relieve ourselves of the pressure of trying to influence external factors that are out of our control by concentrating on what we can manage. The amazing changes that take place when we take charge of our lives are proof of the strength that each of us possesses as well as the transformational power of our decisions.

March 18th

"That which does not kill us makes us stronger." – Friedrich Nietzsche

Although enduring challenging situations might be difficult, they can also result in personal development, knowledge, and a greater appreciation for life's achievements. Keep in mind that the only way we can truly understand the depths of our inner strength and resilience is by experiencing and overcoming hardship. Every obstacle we face serves as a stepping stone on our path to personal development, making us stronger and more able to accept the complexity of life.

March 19th

"Happiness is the highest good" – Aristotle

Above everything else, happiness should be our top priority in life. Keep in mind that happiness is a personal experience, and what makes one person happy may not make another person happy. Accept your individual road to happiness and make your happiness and well-being a top priority in all areas of your life.

March 20th

"The two most important days in your life are the day you are born and the day you find out why." – Mark Twain

Self-discovery and reflection are necessary steps on the path to discovering one's purpose. To find what actually fulfills us, we must reflect on our passions, values, and strengths. Embrace the process of self-discovery and give yourself permission to be led by what makes you happy, sparks your passion, and reflects your values

March 21st

"Do not let the behavior of others destroy your inner peace."
– Dalai Lama

How we react to other people's actions is something we have control over. We can decide not to let their acts disrupt our inner peace. Embrace the training of mindfulness and self-awareness, which enables us to be aware of our responses and consciously react to outside stimuli.

March 22nd

"Be a loner. That gives you time to wonder, to search for the truth. Have holy curiosity. Make your life worth living." – Albert Einstein

Being a "loner," or spending time by oneself, can be beneficial for self-reflection and introspection. One can explore their ideas and feelings when they are alone. It promotes a passion for knowledge and intellectual curiosity.

March 23rd

"You can't put a limit on anything. The more you dream, the farther you get." – Michael Phelps

By having great dreams and not limiting our ambitions, we provide ourselves access to a world of opportunity for personal growth. Dreams serve as a compass, encouraging us to keep going and put in endless effort to achieve our objectives. We challenge ourselves and grow in ways we may not have first believed possible the more we dream big and aim high.

March 24th

"The only thing we have to fear is fear itself." – Franklin D. Roosevelt

This famous quote, spoken by President Franklin D. Roosevelt during the Great Depression in his inaugural address in 1933, has a significant message about the nature of fear and how it affects our lives. It implies that fear itself may provide a substantial challenge for us. When we give into fear, it might paralyze our actions and keep us from achieving our objectives. The only thing we really need to be afraid of is letting fear take over our life and keep us from living to the fullest.

March 25th

"The man who moves a mountain begins by carrying away small stones." – Confucius

It can be overwhelming to work toward ambitious goals but breaking them down into smaller, more doable tasks will enable you to make steady progress over time. It may take a while to move a mountain, but persistent work often leads to success.

March 26th

"Happiness is a state of mind. It's just according to the way you look at things." – Walt Disney Company

Happiness is a mental and emotional state rather than an external event. Our thoughts, viewpoints, and interpretations of life experiences all have an impact on it. Positivity and optimism are behaviors that can increase happiness. Be conscious of the thoughts and beliefs that could prevent happiness, and concentrate on the things that bring you joy and meaning.

March 27th

"Watch your thoughts; they become words. Watch your words; they become actions. Watch your actions; they become habits. Watch your habits; they become character. Watch your character; it becomes your destiny." – Lao Tzu

The course of our lives is influenced by our thoughts, words, and actions. We can try to create a purposeful and fulfilling future by being aware of them. This quote should motivate us to think positively, speak thoughtfully and develop healthy habits. By doing this, we can shape our personalities and create a destiny that is consistent with our goals and ideals.

March 28th

"A day without laughter is a day wasted." – Charlie Chaplin

Cultivate a sense of humor and look for reasons to laugh even when things are difficult. Keep in mind that laughing is not only a response to happiness, but can also make you happy. Make an effort to surround yourself with individuals and things that make you laugh. We may improve the quality of our days and make each moment more significant by embracing laughter and acknowledging its positive effects on our well-being. Laugh with others, enjoy being positive, and treasure the joy that laughing offers.

March 29th

"We are what we repeatedly do. Excellence, then, is not an act, but a habit" – Aristotle

Discipline and consistency in our behavior are necessary for excellence. We can improve our performance and become extraordinary by developing good habits and upholding them. Always keep in mind that excellence is a journey rather than a goal. Accept the journey of self-improvement and practice patience with yourself as you establish fresh habits and move closer to your goals.

March 30th

"He who is not courageous enough to take risks will accomplish nothing in life." – Plato

For one to advance personally and attain goals, courage is an important skill. Without taking chances, people can stagnate and pass up valuable opportunities. Success and greatness frequently come to those who have the courage to take chances, even if they consist of a certain amount of risk.

March 31st

"Without ambition one starts nothing. Without work one finishes nothing. The prize will not be sent to you. You have to win it."
– Ralph Waldo Emerson

We are in charge of our own success. In order to achieve our goals, we must work hard. Achievement will not come from passiveness. While the road to success may not always be easy, the benefits of commitment and dedication are tremendous. Our chances of making our dreams come true rise when we have ambition, value sacrifice, and take ownership of our success.

April 1st

"Curiosity about life in all of its aspects, I think, is still the secret of great creative people." – Leo Burnett

Unlocking one's creative potential and becoming great requires maintaining a curious and inquisitive attitude about life's many elements. Curiosity motivates us to investigate and be receptive to different elements of life. The source of creativity is curiosity.

April 2nd

"Whether you think you can or you think you can't, you're right."
– Henry Ford

Our thoughts can become self-fulfilling prophecies. We are more inclined to put up the effort and take the steps that result in achievement if we have faith in our ability to succeed. A confident and resilient mindset can help us overcome challenges and failures with persistence.

April 3rd

"The brave man is he who overcomes not only his enemies but his pleasures." – Democritus

A truly courageous person must possess self-discipline and the ability to resist indulgent behavior. It takes courage and self-control to be able to say no to temporary pleasures and instant enjoyment. True bravery aligns with having a strong sense of integrity and committing to one's values.

April 4th

"The big lesson in life, baby, is never be scared of anyone or anything."– Frank Sinatra

Living fearlessly enables us to experience life to the fullest and face circumstances with confidence and empowerment. Accept the important lesson of fearlessness and keep in mind that you have the inner strength to deal with anything or anybody who crosses your path.

April 5th

"Life is a succession of lessons which must be lived to be understood." – Helen Keller

Our personal growth and identity are shaped by the lessons we learn throughout life. We must actively engage in and accept the experiences that come our way if we are to properly learn the teachings of life.

April 6th

"Twenty years from now, you will be more disappointed by the things you didn't do than by the ones you did do." – Mark Twain

The most unforgettable events in life are typically the results of taking chances and venturing into the unknown. More powerful than any disappointments we can face when following our goals can be the regret of not going after our dreams or trying new things.

April 7th

"Man is born free, but is everywhere in chains."
– Jean-Jacques Rousseau

Although everyone has a certain amount of natural freedom, different societal, political, and cultural restrictions frequently limit this freedom, creating the feeling that one is "in chains." Finding the right balance between society restrictions and individual freedom is essential.

April 8th

"If you are depressed you are living in the past, if you are anxious you are living in the future. If you are at peace, you are living in the present."
– Lao Tzu

Worrying about the future or focusing on one's past regrets is frequently associated with depression and anxiety. By living in the now, we can let go of our past burdens and future worries and find peace in the here and now. Keep in mind that while it's vital to reflect on the past and make plans for the future, it's also crucial to recognize the beauty and opportunities of the now.

April 9th

"Each day is a little life: every waking and rising a little birth, every fresh morning a little youth, every going to rest and sleep a little death." – Arthur Schopenhauer

Life is made up of a series of interconnected moments, each with its own special meaning. Like a condensed version of the greater human experience, each day offers the possibility of regeneration, growth, and discovery. Life is full of different changes that influence our journey, just as we transition from waking to sleeping and from youth to adulthood. This quote emphasizes this fleeting aspect of life and encourages us to cherish each second and make the most of our experiences.

April 10th

"When it is obvious that goals can't be reached, don't adjust the goals, but adjust the action steps." – Confucius

Adjusting our action steps allows us to find innovative solutions to move beyond barriers in our way to success. Be willing to reevaluate and modify the course of action if a particular approach is not producing the expected outcomes. Keep in mind that progress is frequently not a straight line and that setbacks are a normal part of the path to success. We can develop fresh and creative approaches to accomplish our goals by being open to adapt our action steps. Be persistent in your goals, but also flexible enough to shift course as necessary.

April 11th

"My mission in life is not merely to survive, but to thrive; and to do so with some passion, some compassion, some humor, and some style."
— *Maya Angelou*

You may design a life that is both gratifying and has a beneficial impact on others around you by living with purpose, passion, compassion, humor, and style. Accept your individual journey, rejoice in each moment, and strive to live a life that is both prosperous and profoundly meaningful.

April 12th

"The mind is everything. What you think you become." – *Buddha*

The mind acts as a powerful creator of our reality, acting as the driving force behind our experiences and behaviors. We may bring about positive changes in our own lives by establishing a positive and constructive mindset. Make use of this knowledge of the mind's capacity to motivate personal development and self-improvement. Realize that the thoughts you choose to entertain can help you to mold your own story and create the life you want.

April 13th

"If we don't change, we don't grow. If we don't grow, we aren't really living." – *Gail Sheehy*

Keep in mind that growth is not always simple and may require you to leave your comfort zone. However, the benefits of personal growth and self-discovery make the work worthwhile. With a growth mindset, embrace life's path and actively seek out new opportunities for learning. Be flexible, develop resilience, and adjust to life's ever-changing circumstances.

April 14th

"One word frees us of all the weight and pain in life, that word is Love."
— *Sophocles*

Love has the amazing power to alleviate burdens, soothe suffering, and create a sense of freedom and wholeness. Develop love in your interactions with others by being kind, sympathetic, and understanding. Do not forget to love yourself as well, acknowledge your worth and value as a person, and cultivate self-love and compassion.

April 15th

"Everything you've ever wanted is on the other side of fear."
— *George Addair*

Although fear is a normal emotion, we can't let it control our decisions and actions. Recognize your fears, but don't let them stop you. In order to achieve your goals, step outside of your comfort zone.

April 16th

"Freedom is the only worthy goal in life. It is won by disregarding things that lie beyond our control." — *Epictetus*

True freedom comes from concentrating on what we can control and letting go of ties to things that are beyond our power. Focus on the aspects of your life that you have control over, such as your thoughts, actions, and responses to difficulties. Keep in mind that we often have little control over the external world or the behavior of other individuals. We can achieve tranquility and freedom from unnecessary obligations by letting go of the desire to control the uncontrollable.

April 17th

"When another blames you or hates you, or people voice similar criticisms, go to their souls, penetrate inside and see what sort of people they are. You will realize that there is no need to be racked with anxiety that they should hold any particular opinion about you."
– Marcus Aurelius, Meditations

Recognize the potential motivations underlying other people's opinions and actions and keep in mind that they could not be accurate reflections of our genuine character or worth. People's comments might not be an assessment of our value as individuals, but rather a reflection of their own personal struggles. Be mindful of constructive criticism and learn from it, but avoid being burdened by baseless criticism or hate.

April 18th

"Everyone thinks of changing the world, but no one thinks of changing himself." – Leo Tolstoy

Introspection and personal development are the first steps on the route to bringing a positive change in the world. Accept trials and failures as chances for learning and growth, and rejoice in the progress you make along the road. Personal growth is a continuous process.

April 19th

"Life is like a piano. What you get out of it depends on how you play it."
– Albert Einstein

Just as the artistry and talent of a pianist determine the melody that is generated, the quality and course of our lives are determined by our decisions, actions, and attitudes. Think about the melodies you want to compose in your life, the objectives you want to accomplish, and the principles you want to uphold. We have a blank canvas in life to create our own songs on. If you seize the chance to play the piano of your life with passion, purpose, and love, you will create a lovely and harmonious symphony that speaks to your heart.

April 20th

"If you look for perfection, you'll never be content." – Leo Tolstoy, Anna Karenina

The pursuit of perfection can frequently result in unhappiness and discontentment. The appreciation of our present and past accomplishments might be overshadowed by the search for an unrealistic ideal. Greater peace and contentment could be achieved by accepting flaws as a normal aspect of life.

April 21st

"And those who were seen dancing were thought to be insane by those who could not hear the music."– Friedrich Nietzsche

Depending on their viewpoints and levels of awareness, different people have unique ways of seeing and understanding the world. Living genuinely requires embracing one's actual self and desires, even while doing so may cause one to be seen as unusual or different. Certain facets of life and experiences may only be appreciated by those who are open to them, just as music can only be heard by those who are tuned in to it.

April 22nd

"To live is the rarest thing in the world. Most people exist, that is all." – Oscar Wilde

We can only completely appreciate life's richness when we are in the present and involved in all that we do. Become present in the moment, look for new opportunities, and follow your passions to find happiness and contentment. The journey of actually living is a continual process, and life is a priceless gift. When you make the decision to live your life with determination, purpose, and a sense of adventure, you'll discover that the rare beauty of a fully lived life unfolds in front of you.

April 23rd

"If you spend your whole life waiting for the storm, you'll never enjoy the sunshine." – Morris West

You can develop resilience and a sense of gratitude that aids you in getting through difficult times by making the decision to appreciate the sunshine despite the uncertainties. Never forget that no matter what happens outside of you, you have the power to experience joy and happiness.

April 24th

"Whatever the mind of man can conceive and believe, it can achieve."
– Napoleon Hill

One of the most important forces driving people toward their goals is the conviction that success is possible. Visualize your goals and have faith that you can achieve them. This conviction can serve as an incentive for you to work consistently and purposefully in the direction of your goals.

April 25th

"Whatever your life's work is, do it well. A man should do his job so well that the living, the dead, and the unborn could do it no better.
– Martin Luther King Jr.

When one constantly strives to accomplish their work with the highest level of expertise, integrity, and commitment, they will find true fulfillment and success. A sense of achievement and a meaningful existence can come from taking pride in your profession and dedicating yourself to it.

April 26th

"No man's knowledge here can go beyond his experience"
– John Locke

We can keep deepening our understanding and enhancing our lives by actively seeking out new experiences and remaining open to various points of view. Look for chances to interact with others with different perspectives, expand your horizons, and embrace new challenges.

April 27th

"Anyone who holds a true opinion without understanding is like a blind man on the right road." – Socrates

Simply adopting an opinion without fully understanding it can result in a limited and underdeveloped perspective. More educated thoughts result from critical thinking and an effort to understand the motivations behind opinions.

April 28th

"Keep smiling, because life is a beautiful thing and there's so much to smile about." – Marilyn Monroe

There are endless reasons to smile and be happy, even in trying circumstances. Focusing on the good things in life can improve our general wellbeing and mentality. Take time to appreciate the beauty all around you – the warmth of the sun, and the laughter of loved ones, the joy that comes from simple pleasures.

April 29th

"I think therefore I am" ("Cogito, ergo sum") – René Descartes

A sense of personal identity is influenced by thinking and self-awareness. Consider the effects of self-awareness and how our thoughts influence how we perceive ourselves. The phrase "I think therefore I am" is ultimately meant to serve as a reminder of the profound relationship between thought, awareness, and the very nature of our being.

April 30th

"An ounce of action is worth a ton of theory." – Ralph Waldo Emerson

Practical actions and real-world experiences are more valuable and credible than speculative concepts. Sometimes, making that first move is more important than continuously strategizing and planning. Although theoretical knowledge is important, real change is only achieved by application of that knowledge.

May 1st

"Life is pretty simple: You do some stuff. Most fails. Some works. You do more of what works. If it works big, others quickly copy it. Then you do something else. The trick is in doing something else."
– Leonardo da Vinci

In life, there are many things to try, some of which might not produce the desired results. Failures present chances for growth and learning. When you come upon something effective, concentrate on it and attempt to make it more powerful. As success is demonstrated, others might copy it. One must always change and look for new opportunities in order to stay ahead. The quote's fundamental principle is that we should always be learning, investigating new ideas, and never being too comfortable.

May 2nd

"Go confidently in the direction of your dreams! Live the life you've imagined." – Henry David Thoreau

Take advantage of the possibilities that present themselves and work persistently to create the life you envision. As you work toward your goals, embrace a sense of confidence, understanding that difficulties are a necessary part of the trip. Realize that your goals are worthwhile and deserving of pursuit.

May 3rd

"Knowing others is intelligence; knowing yourself is true wisdom. Mastering others is strength; mastering yourself is true power."
– Lao Tzu

Understanding others is valuable, but mastering yourself is a more extensive form of personal development. Possessing control over your own thoughts, actions, and decisions gives you true power. Spend some time considering your own qualities, flaws, and morals. Develop emotional intelligence and exercise self-control in difficult circumstances.

May 4th

"The only impossible journey is the one you never begin."
– Tony Robbins

Once we start, even the most challenging goals become attainable. Take that important initial step toward your goals to overcome the feeling of fear and doubt. Keep in mind that progress frequently begins with simple, brief actions that add up over time.

May 5th

"If you can do what you do best and be happy, you're further along in life than most people." – Leonardo DiCaprio

True success is defined by the joy and happiness you gain from your actions rather than just by your external accomplishments. Remember that the road to fulfillment is different for everyone, and combining your interests and strengths makes you stand out. Prioritize activities that spark your interest and excitement and strive for a harmonious balance between your strengths and your passions.

May 6th

"The only way to deal with fear is to face it." – Seneca

Although it can be uncomfortable or even intimidating, embracing fear is an essential step in getting past its restrictions. Accept the fact that facing fear can result in good development, increased self-awareness, and the chance to accomplish objectives that might have otherwise seemed unattainable.

May 7th

"Be where you are; otherwise you will miss your life." – Buddha

By fully focusing on the present, we can let go of any distractions that could otherwise keep us from experiencing life's full potential. Accept the idea of "being where you are" and make an effort to let go of any anxieties, concerns, or regrets that might cause you to lose sight of the moment.

May 8th

"The biggest risk is not taking any risk. In a world that is changing quickly, the only strategy that is guaranteed to fail is not taking risks."
– Mark Zuckerberg

In a world where change is constant, taking risks becomes crucial for adaptation and development. Keep in mind that not all risks involve careless behavior; calculated risks necessitate careful planning and preparation. Venturing beyond your comfort zone and heading into unfamiliar territory is frequently where you will find the possibility for development, innovation, and success.

May 9th

"Change the way you look at things and the things you look at change."
– Wayne W. Dyer

Our perceptions influence our reality, and changing our viewpoint can result in a different reality. You can find underlying insights, solve issues, and develop feelings of gratitude and contentment by deliberately choosing to look at circumstances from different perspectives. You have the ability to change your reality by changing the lens through which you view things.

May 10th

"Be not afraid of life. Believe that life is worth living, and your belief will help create the fact." – William James

A trigger for growth and positive transformation can be found in the conviction that life is valuable. Adopting the perspective that life is precious encourages optimism and resilience in the face of difficulties. The quote encourages us to seize opportunities, take chances, and fully engage in life.

May 11th

"We suffer more often in imagination than in reality"
– Lucius Annaeus Seneca

Through excessive thinking and imagination, our minds have an inclination to exaggerate problems. Sometimes the suffering we expect doesn't match the reality of the circumstance. Realizing that imagined suffering might be more severe than actual suffering can help us build resilience and coping mechanisms. Being present and grounded in reality can also help reduce unnecessary suffering brought on by the imagination.

May 12th

"When you are offended at any man's fault, turn to yourself and study your own failings. Then you will forget your anger." – Epictetus

Recognizing our own flaws might help us empathize with others. Anger can be reduced by turning the attention from external to internal reflection. We can create healthier relationships, ease tensions, and encourage a more peaceful and compassionate way of dealing with others by realizing and correcting our own imperfections.

May 13th

"If it is not right do not do it; if it is not true do not say it."
– Marcus Aurelius, Meditations

Always ask yourself if what you're about to do or say is right or true before acting or speaking. Adopt a commitment to honesty, and let this value direct how you interact with people and how you affect the world.

May 14th

"Look closely. The beautiful may be small."– Immanuel Kant

Beauty is not only found in huge or prominent elements, it can also be found in the subtle and modest. Let's give ourselves permission to feel more deeply connected to the world and to have a greater appreciation for the beauty that is all around us, whether it is in relationships, nature, art, or ordinary moments.

May 15th

"Treat your men as you would your own beloved sons. And they will follow you into the deepest valley." – Sun Tzu, The Art of War

Respect, compassion, and a strong feeling of responsibility for the people you are in charge of should be the foundation of good leadership. Respecting and being kind to others encourages loyalty and harmony. Setting a good example and treating others the way you want to be treated are essential components of effective leadership.

May 16th

"Everything you say should be true, but not everything true should be said." – Voltaire

While being truthful is fundamental, it's also important to take the timing and context of some truths into account. Understanding that some truths could be unnecessary or hurtful promotes empathy and emotional intelligence in conversation.

May 17th

"Find people who will make you better." – Michelle Obama

It is very important to make smart choices when selecting our social group because it can impact who we become. We can create an environment that supports our personal and professional development by surrounding ourselves with like-minded, positive, and ambitious people.

May 18th

"Thinking is difficult, that's why most people judge." – C.G. Jung

Passing judgment might be a quicker and easier response than engaging in critical and objective thinking. Before making snap decisions about other people or difficult situations, let's pause. Take on the challenge of thinking carefully, taking into account different points of view, and attempting to truly understand before drawing conclusions.

May 19th

"Good character is not formed in a week or a month. It is created little by little, day by day. Protracted and patient effort is needed to develop good character." – Heraclitus

The same way that a sculpture is gradually formed, excellent character is developed through regular, consistent acts and decisions. We can progressively develop a strong and admirable character that is a tribute to our ideals and principles by regularly exhibiting integrity, generosity, perseverance, and other desirable traits. Character development is a continuous process that shows a dedication to persistent personal improvement.

May 20th

"Be faithful to that which exists within yourself." – André Gide

Being faithful to oneself demonstrates respect and acceptance of oneself, which promotes a sense of empowerment and confidence. You can develop a sense of inner peace, fulfillment, and a life that reflects your originality and uniqueness by being true to your own objectives and ideals.

May 21st

"No one can construct for you the bridge upon which precisely you must cross the stream of life, no one but you yourself alone."
– Friedrich Nietzsche

Independent decision-making and problem-solving build resilience and personal growth. The journey that each person chooses to follow is specific to their own experiences, values, and objectives. You take charge of your life and become the creator of your own destiny when you realize that only you have the power to build your bridge.

May 22nd

"A man who dares to waste one hour of time has not discovered the value of life." – Charles Darwin

Every moment that passes cannot be regained as time is limited. The value of life is directly related to how we use our time, and wasting it lowers the quality of our existence. Every hour offers opportunities for development, productivity, and fulfilling experiences; neglecting to see this potential is a lost opportunity. Seizing chances, following passions, and making constructive contributions to our own well-being and the world around us are all part of embracing the value of life.

May 23rd

"Silence is better than unmeaning words." – Pythagoras

Our thoughts, feelings, and objectives can be expressed through communication, which is a strong instrument. However, not every concept or every situation calls for verbal expression. In fact, speaking without giving it significant thought can result in misunderstanding, confusion, or even harm. Pick your words carefully.

May 24th

"Whoever will be free must make himself free. Freedom is no fairy gift to fall into a man's lap. What is freedom? To have the will to be responsible for one's self." – Max Stirner

We can develop a stronger sense of freedom and strength by exercising our autonomy, making thoughtful decisions, and taking responsibility for our actions. True freedom comes from having the strength to take charge of our lives and direct ourselves in a manner consistent with our goals and moral principles.

May 25th

"Apply yourself both now and in the next life. Without effort, you cannot be prosperous. Though the land be good, you cannot have an abundant crop without cultivation." – Plato

We do not receive success and fortune on a silver platter. Instead, they are the results of our efforts, perseverance, and dedication. We must apply ourselves in every aspect of life, including work, relationships, and personal development. We can turn potential into achievement by working hard and remaining persistent.

May 26th

"Don't be afraid to give up the good to go for the great."
– John D. Rockefeller

When there may be potential for something even better, are we clinging onto something "good" out of fear or complacency? Although it frequently takes determination and courage to embrace change and strive for greatness, the potential rewards can result in a more meaningful and happy life path.

May 27th

"The two most powerful warriors are patience and time."– Leo Tolstoy

Success often involves adopting a long-term perspective and understanding that accomplishments may not be evident right away. Patience is a vital trait, which enables people to overcome obstacles and failures with resiliency and perseverance. The capacity to endure and persist through time is a powerful quality that can result in important success.

May 28th

"Life is what happens when you're busy making other plans."
– John Lennon

While making future plans is important, it's also crucial to maintain balance and avoid being so preoccupied with the future that we overlook the beauty of our current life. The most significant moments in life happen when we are totally present and involved, embracing the moment as it unfolds before us.

May 29th

"There is only one way to avoid criticism: do nothing, say nothing, and be nothing." – Aristotle

Life will inevitably include criticism, especially for people who take chances, express themselves, and work hard to succeed. Even if it means facing judgment, we should be genuine and present in our lives. Instead of trying to escape criticism, let's concentrate on upholding our principles, following our passions, and carrying on with our goals in our own special way.

May 30th

"It's not your job to like me; it's mine." – Byron Katie

Self-acceptance and self-worth shouldn't be based on the opinions or approval of others. The responsibility for one's own self-esteem and self-perception is emphasized in this quote. You relieve yourself of the stress of perpetual approval seeking by realizing that other people's opinions are not an indicator of your value.

May 31st

"It is during our darkest moments that we must focus to see the light."
– Aristotle

Our inner strength, determination, and attitude determine our ability to move through challenging circumstances. The quote encourages us to change our perspective and direct our attention toward looking for the "light" rather than giving in to hopelessness. Keep in mind that there is always a chance for light and change, even at our darkest times.

June 1st

"What the superior man seeks is in himself; what the small man seeks is in others." – Confucius

With a focus on the importance of self-awareness and self-improvement, the superior person seeks inner characteristics, strengths, and virtues as a source of fulfillment and growth. The small-minded individual puts their pleasure and sense of worth in the hands of other people, relying on others for approval.

June 2nd

"Most of the important things in the world have been accomplished by people who have kept on trying when there seemed to be no hope at all. – Dale Carnegie

Moments of doubt or difficulties do not always signify failure; rather, they can present possibilities for progress. Success usually demands continuous commitment and the ability to persevere in the face of difficulty.

June 3rd

"In three words, I can sum up everything I've learned about life: it goes on." – Robert Frost

Although life has its ups and downs, it has the natural ability to persist and move forward in spite of obstacles and changes. Life goes on, and so do we. May we discover the power within ourselves to continue and handle whatever comes our way.

June 4th

"The more man meditates upon good thoughts, the better will be his world and the world at large." – Confucius

Positive thoughts and attitudes can create a ripple effect. Our thoughts affect how we see the world, as well as how we feel, behave, and interact with others. We have the power to manifest a reality that is more uplifting and harmonious through deliberate, conscious thought.

June 5th

"Don't let anyone tell you what you can't do. Follow your dreams and persist." – Barack Obama

We must reject the restrictions set by other people and overcome any unfavorable influences or critics. Don't let people set limitations on your potential or define your abilities. Trust your instincts and have faith in what you can do. Embrace your inner strength, overcome obstacles, and maintain a commitment to your goals.

June 6th

"The secret of getting ahead is getting started." – Mark Twain

The hardest part is often the beginning. Once you get going, you gain momentum, which makes it simpler to carry on and finish what you started. The first step in overcoming any mental or emotional barriers that may be preventing you from moving forward is to begin a work or activity. Progress cannot be made without that first step. Every big achievement starts with the initial decision to start.

June 7th

"The first and greatest victory is to conquer yourself." – Plato

Self-discipline is a skill that must be mastered in order to conquer oneself and lead a balanced life. The most challenging battles are usually the ones that must be won inside of oneself – overcoming fears, doubts, and bad habits. It is crucial to gain control of your internal battles before obtaining exterior successes.

June 8th

"To reach a port, we must sail – sail, not tie at anchor – sail, not drift." – Franklin D. Roosevelt

Drifting or tying at anchor denotes inaction and stagnation. Sailing is a metaphor for forward movement and progress. Although sailing may require navigating through tough waters where we encounter difficulties and uncertainty, it is a crucial step in getting to our intended ports.

June 9th

"It is difficult to find happiness within oneself, but it is impossible to find it anywhere else." – Arthur Schopenhauer

While temporary influences from the outside world may affect our mood, true happiness ultimately comes from within. Externally pursuing happiness, such as through material goods or other people's approval, might produce momentary gratification but not long-term fulfillment. The source of real happiness is within us; it comes from our own views, thoughts, and attitudes.

June 10th

"A person's worth is measured by the worth of what he values."
— Marcus Aurelius, Meditations

Our views, ideals, and what we hold dear are reflected in our values. They sculpt our identities and direct our behavior. The significance and integrity of one's values establish their worth. Finding meaning and joy in life comes from making decisions that are consistent with what we value.

June 11th

"I have learned to seek my happiness by limiting my desires, rather than in attempting to satisfy them." *— John Stuart Mill*

True happiness does not only depend on external acquisitions; it also comes from within. We can build a sense of happiness that comes from inside by engaging in thoughtful and deliberate living, which results in a more well-balanced and satisfying life.

June 12th

"What we fear doing most is usually what we most need to do.
— Tim Ferriss

Usually, the exact things or situations we fear the most have the greatest potential to advance our growth and happiness. By facing our fears, we can get over constraints that might be preventing us from realizing our full potential.

June 13th

"Everyone has inside of him a piece of good news. The good news is that you don't know how great you can be! How much you can love! What you can accomplish! And what your potential is!" – Anne Frank

Every one of us has hidden talents and potential that we may not even be aware of. We have the capacity to achieve great things and to love deeply in ways that go beyond what we now understand. Our potential is infinite. Understanding our inherent potential can give us the courage to take on challenges, make big plans, and pursue personal development.

June 14th

"The happiness of your life depends upon the quality of your thoughts."
– Marcus Aurelius

Our perspective on life is significantly shaped by the thoughts we have. Greater happiness and contentment can result from having a good and constructive mindset. Being conscious of our thinking patterns enables us to identify and alter unpleasant or damaging thoughts, promoting a more positive state of mind. Our thoughts affect our emotions, thus focusing on positive thoughts can improve our emotional health.

June 15th

"It never ceases to amaze me: we all love ourselves more than other people, but care more about their opinion than our own."
– Marcus Aurelius, Meditations

Although we naturally love ourselves, we frequently allow the opinions of others to undermine our self-assurance. We should think about why we value other people's opinions over our own, as well as the effect this has on our self-confidence. Although the opinions of others might be insightful, our sense of self-worth and happiness should ultimately come from within and be based on our own genuine perception of who we are.

June 16th

"A man must be big enough to admit his mistakes, smart enough to profit from them, and strong enough to correct them. — John C. Maxwell

A sign of intelligence is seeing mistakes as chances for development and learning. The lessons we learn from our mistakes help us grow in knowledge and as people. Making corrections shows perseverance and resilience. We may continue to develop, grow, and ultimately improve into better versions of ourselves by admitting and fixing our mistakes.

June 17th

"One who makes himself a worm cannot complain afterwards if people step on him."– Immanuel Kant

Someone should not be surprised if others treat them disrespectfully or take advantage of them if they present themselves as weak, submissive, or lacking in self-confidence (expressed figuratively as a worm). People are more likely to respect people who radiate strength and respect for themselves.

June 18th

"Educating the mind without educating the heart is no education at all." – Aristotle

The development of emotional intelligence, empathy, compassion, and a sense of morality are all involved in "educating the heart." Getting a well-rounded education involves more than just learning information. It aims to develop empathy, compassion, and a firm ethical foundation.

June 19th

"The first method for estimating the intelligence of a ruler is to look at the men he has around him." – Niccolò Machiavelli, The Prince

People who share their intellectual curiosity, desire for success, and love for learning tend to attract intelligent people. Having a network of talented and smart individuals around you may imply that you have the capacity to build meaningful connections, collaborate well, and value different viewpoints.

June 20th

"It does not matter how slowly you go as long as you do not stop."
– Confucius

No matter what size, every step adds up to the whole journey. We must keep going forward, no matter how slowly, whether we are chasing personal objectives, career aspirations, or just trying to improve ourselves. We are moving forward as long as we stay focused and keep taking actions, regardless of how small.

June 21st

"Life is what we make it and how we make it – whether we realize it or not." – Napoleon Hill

Every choice we make, every attitude we adopt, and every action we take affects the overall direction and quality of our life, whether we are conscious of it or not. We have the ability to create our own destinies and craft our own narratives. Even in the face of difficulties or unforeseen situations, our actions and choices have the power to influence how our journey turns out.

June 22nd

"If they spit at you behind your back it means you're ahead of them."
– Confucius

People who are not on the same level as you may be unfriendly or jealous of you if you are ahead of them. It's okay if not everyone acknowledges or supports your accomplishments. In fact, coming up against opposition may indicate that you're headed in the right direction. Maintain your self-assurance, have faith in your path, and use any difficulties or setbacks as motivation for further development and success.

June 23rd

"I have not failed. I've just found 10,000 ways that won't work."
– Thomas Edison

This quote promotes a growth mindset by portraying failure as a path toward discovery and improvement. It inspires us to rise to the occasion, adjust, and keep persistently pursuing our objectives. Every unsuccessful attempt is a chance to learn important lessons, alter our strategy, and get closer to success.

June 24th

"Anyone can become angry – that is easy, but to be angry with the right person at the right time, and for the right purpose and in the right way – that is not within everyone's power and that is not easy." – Aristotle

Even though everyone can experience anger, the trick is knowing how to manage it responsibly and constructively. Impulsive or in-the-moment reactions can result in misunderstandings and undesirable outcomes. It's important to comprehend why you feel this way and what you expect to accomplish by expressing your feelings. Better results can be achieved by approaching the matter with respect, empathy, and effective communication than by being confrontational or expressing anger in a detrimental way.

June 25th

"I never dreamed about success. I worked for it." – Estée Lauder

Success is not given to you for free; you must work hard, be determined, and be willing to face obstacles in order to achieve it. Success is a result of hard work, perseverance, and resilience. It's not given away by chance or wishful thinking.

June 26th

"Insanity: Doing the same thing over and over again and expecting different results." – Albert Einstein

Frustration and disappointment might emerge from consistently anticipating different outcomes from the same acts. By being aware of this tendency, we may proactively change our strategy and adopt a more constructive mindset. Whether our acts were effective or unsuccessful, we must learn from them and apply the lessons to the future.

June 27th

"If what you have seems insufficient to you, then though you possess the world, you will yet be miserable." – Seneca

Our ability to see the worth and fulfillment in what we currently have, as well as our personal perspective, determine our level of contentment. The careful balance of embracing gratitude and acknowledging what we already have while still pursuing our goals generates true happiness.

June 28th

"We have two ears and one mouth so that we can listen twice as much as we speak." – Epictetus

We give ourselves the opportunity for growth and learning by attentively listening. We broaden our knowledge and become more receptive to new ideas. This not only improves our comprehension of those around us but also encourages stronger ties and more fulfilling connections.

June 29th

"The way to get started is to quit talking and begin doing." – Walt Disney

This highlights the inclination of many of us to overthink, plan, or talk about our ideas without actually taking action to make them a reality. Progress can frequently be affected by procrastination and indecision, which keeps us from accomplishing our objectives or realizing our visions.

June 30th

"All change is hard at first, messy in the middle and gorgeous at the end." – Robin Sharma

As we adjust to new situations or routines, the beginning of any change or transformation can be difficult and demanding. While we make our way through the process during the middle phase of change, there are frequent times of tension, uncertainty, and confusion. Our efforts generate fruit towards the conclusion of the journey, giving us a sense of accomplishment and fulfillment. We have the chance to see the beauty that results from our work and dedication by persevering through the difficulties and doubts.

July 1st

"Don't limit yourself. Many people limit themselves to what they think they can do. You can go as far as your mind lets you. What you believe, remember, you can achieve." – Mary Kay Ash

We unintentionally prevent ourselves from realizing our full potential if we set ourselves up for failure by questioning our talents or having low expectations.Our actions and decisions are shaped by our beliefs. We are more likely to take risks, seize opportunities, and persevere in the face of adversity when we have faith in our skills and an optimistic perspective. On the other hand, we might pass up opportunities for development and success if we doubt ourselves or let fear rule our thinking.

July 2nd

"Concern should drive us into action and not into a depression. No man is free who cannot control himself."– Pythagoras

We must turn our worries into proactive actions rather than letting them lead us to feel hopeless or depressed. We are better able to deal with difficulties and use them as opportunities for personal development when we are able to control our impulses and emotions.

July 3rd

"Nothing, to my way of thinking, is a better proof of a well ordered mind than a man's ability to stop just where he is and pass some time in his own company."– Seneca

In a world that frequently favors constant activity and external stimulus, the capacity to find comfort and contentment in one's own thoughts is in fact a testimonial to a well-balanced and harmonious mind. It is possible to learn more about yourself, engage in introspection, and gain a deeper comprehension of your ideas and feelings by pausing to think, reflect, and enjoy your own company. Developing a meaningful inner life is what leads to actual fulfillment rather than relying simply on external pursuits.

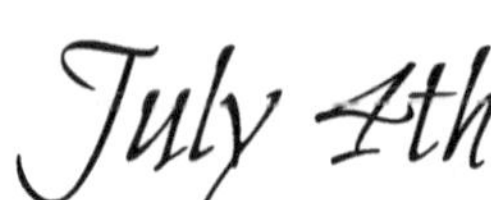

July 4th

"Happiness and freedom begin with one principle. Some things are within your control and some are not." – Epictetus

We can influence our own well-being and produce beneficial results by concentrating our attention and efforts on the things that are within our control – our thoughts, actions, and attitudes. At the same time, realizing that there are external elements that are out of our control enables us to let go of unnecessary worry and anxiety.

July 5th

"The best and most beautiful things in the world cannot be seen or even heard, but must be felt with the heart." – Helen Keller

It's in the whispers of encouragement, the genuine smiles, the moments of shared happiness that we truly experience life's magnificence. So, let us listen with our hearts, feel with our souls, and embrace the profound beauty that transcends the boundaries of the visible and the audible.

July 6th

"When everything seems to be going against you, remember that the airplane takes off against the wind, not with it." – Henry Ford

Just as an airplane takes off against the wind's resistance, our own progress and growth often requires pushing past difficulties. Our genuine strength and resilience are put to the test during these times of adversity. Instead of being discouraged by setbacks, we can be inspired by the notion that conquering obstacles is what propels us ahead.

July 7th

"The educated differ from the uneducated as much as the living from the dead." – Aristotle

Education is more than just learning information; it is also about awakening the mind, extending views, and fostering critical thinking. The educated are mentally alive, actively participating in the search of understanding and wisdom, just as the living are vibrant and involved with the world around them.

July 8th

"Don't be overheard complaining ... not even to yourself." – Marcus Aurelius, Meditations

Even when done in private, complaining can have a subtle effect on our mindset and outlook on life. The quote encourages us to focus on solutions rather than problems by asking us not to be overheard complaining. It promotes the idea that we should focus our attention on positive acts and thoughts rather than negative self-talk.

July 9th

"Don't judge each day by the harvest you reap but by the seeds that you plant." – Robert Louis Stevenson

Just as a farmer does not judge their success solely by the crops they harvest, but also by the time and effort they put into planting and nurturing seeds, our everyday activities and efforts are extremely important. We can create a meaningful and fulfilling life by continually planting positive "seeds" through our acts, kindness, and hard work, regardless of the immediate outcomes we encounter.

July 10th

"Your brain is the most important organ in your body, and what happens in it determines what you think and feel, say and do."
— *Rick Hanson*

We may positively influence every aspect of our life and make meaningful contributions to our own growth and the well-being of people around us by nurturing our brain health, cultivating happy thoughts, and practicing mindfulness.

July 11th

"The most effective way to do it is to do it." — *Amelia Earhart*

The driving force for advancement is action. We frequently get caught up in planning, analyzing, and looking for the "perfect" strategy, when the most direct path to success is simply to begin. Action produces results, and the journey of a thousand miles starts with the first step.

July 12th

"Don't let yesterday take up too much of today." — *Will Rogers*

Concentrate on the present rather than the past. It's normal to think back on past experiences, but allowing them to consume our thoughts and emotions can hinder our progress and enjoyment of the present. We liberate ourselves to completely engage with the opportunities and possibilities that exist today by letting go of regrets, mistakes, or missed opportunities.

July 13th

"It is impossible to live without failing at something, unless you live so cautiously that you might as well not have lived at all – in which case, you fail by default." – J.K. Rowling

Failure is not something to be feared or avoided; rather, it is a necessary and natural part of growth and progress. Living cautiously and avoiding risks may appear to be a means to avoid failure at first, but it eventually leads to a life devoid of significant experiences and accomplishments.

July 14th

"Everything is hard before it is easy."
– Johann Wolfgang von Goethe

When we first encounter something unfamiliar or complex, it might feel hard and overwhelming. However, with commitment, practice, and perseverance, we progressively gain skill and knowledge, and what was difficult becomes more manageable.

July 15th

"Keep your face to the sunshine and you can never see the shadow."
– Helen Keller

The metaphor of keeping one's face to the sun represents an optimistic and hopeful mindset. It urges us to focus on the positive aspects of life, realizing that barriers and hardships will always exist, but choosing not to be consumed by them. Just as a sunflower turns towards the sun to thrive, this phrase encourages us to orient ourselves towards positivity.

July 16th

"For every minute you are angry you lose sixty seconds of happiness."
– Ralph Waldo Emerson

This quote encourages us to evaluate the opportunity cost of being angry, since it deprives us of the potential joy and positivity that such times could offer. By allowing anger to control our actions and thoughts, we unintentionally sacrifice the possibility for happiness that resides in every passing second. While it is difficult to imagine a life free of anger, this quote encourages us to reduce its hold on us, allowing us to focus our attention on other gratifying and pleasant experiences.

July 17th

"He is a wise man who does not grieve for the things which he has not, but rejoices for those which he has." – Epictetus

It takes a certain amount of wisdom to turn our focus away from what is missing and toward the richness and joy that surround us. By teaching ourselves to see and appreciate the abundance in our lives, we cultivate a sense of fulfillment that is not dependent on other things.

July 18th

"Don't let your happiness depend on something you may lose."
– C.S. Lewis

Relying on external sources for our happiness, whether they are material possessions, relationships, or accomplishments, can lead to a delicate feeling of contentment that crumbles when those external variables become absent. This quote invites us to look within ourselves for a deeper and more enduring source of happiness. It encourages us to seek joy, contentment, and tranquility from essentially stable and controllable sources, such as our attitudes, perspectives, and ideals. By doing so, we strengthen our resistance to life's ups and downs and become less vulnerable to the inevitable changes that occur around us.

July 19th

"The safest way to get what you want is to deserve what you want."
- Charlie T. Munger

Our efforts, skills, and character all play a direct role in what we achieve. To attain your goals, concentrate on becoming the person capable of attracting those aspirations. Put in the effort, have faith in your own worth, and witness how you not only will get what you want but you will truly deserve it.

July 20th

"Some of us think holding on makes us strong; but sometimes it is letting go." – Herman Hesse

While it is important to persevere in the face of adversity, there are times when clinging to something – whether it is a relationship, an attachment, a belief, or a previous mistake – can actually be detrimental to our well-being and growth. In such cases, letting go reveals a different sort of strength – the power to let go of what no longer serves us.

July 21st

"We rise by lifting others." – Robert Ingersoll

When we lend a helping hand, share expertise, or offer encouragement to others, we not only improve their well-being but also produce a positive ripple effect. We develop an environment of mutual support and collaboration by assisting others to advance, which ultimately improves our own sense of purpose and fulfillment.

July 22nd

"You will never do anything in this world without courage. It is the greatest quality of the mind next to honor." – Aristotle

While many factors contribute to success, courage stands out as an essential attribute that allows us to overcome obstacles, follow our goals, and uphold our ideals. Without courage, we may be unwilling to step outside of our comfort zones or face frightening challenges. Whether it's establishing a new business, standing up for what we believe in, or confronting unpleasant situations, courage allows us to continue forward in the face of fear and uncertainty.

July 23rd

"People often say that motivation doesn't last. Well, neither does bathing. That's why we recommend it daily." – Zig Ziglar

It is not an effective approach to wait for motivation to arise or to expect it to stay indefinitely. Just like we don't skip regular hygienic practices since we know they won't last forever, we also shouldn't neglect our efforts to stay motivated. Instead, we should deliberately seek out sources of inspiration, create goals, and engage in actions that restore our enthusiasm and drive on a regular basis.

July 24th

"Action may not always bring happiness, but there is no happiness without action." – William James

Happiness is the product of our decisions, efforts, and deeds. The quote encourages us to acknowledge that obtaining happiness demands taking initiative and actively participating in life. Activities that are in line with our values, interests, and aspirations can provide us with a sense of purpose, accomplishment, and joy.

July 25th

"Never think of pain or danger or enemies a moment longer than is necessary to fight them." – Ayn Rand

Rather than becoming overwhelmed or consumed by negative thoughts about pain, danger, or adversaries, we must redirect our focus to proactive steps for dealing with those issues. When faced with challenges, it is essential to keep a strategic and efficient mindset rather than concentrating on them unnecessarily.

July 26th

"Knowing yourself is the beginning of all wisdom." – Aristotle

True wisdom and meaningful life experiences begin with a thorough awareness of one's own thoughts, feelings, motivations, strengths, and limitations. It is difficult to make informed decisions, create meaningful goals, and navigate through life's difficulties without a clear understanding of who we are, our beliefs, and our values. Self-awareness serves as a compass, directing us toward decisions and pathways that are consistent with our real selves.

July 27th

"We can choose courage or we can choose comfort, but we can't have both. Not at the same time. – Brené Brown

To truly embrace courage and all of its opportunities, we need to leave the security of our comfort zones. When we prioritize comfort, we risk missing out on the transforming experiences that come from confronting obstacles.

July 28th

"If you only read the books that everyone else is reading, you can only think what everyone else is thinking." - Haruki Murakami

Venturing beyond the beaten path is often necessary to stand out in life. If all you do is follow the crowd, your actions and ideas may become stale. You have to be willing to take risks and venture into new territory. Dare to be different and let your individuality shape a narrative that resonates with your originality.

July 29th

"Love all, trust a few, do wrong to none." – William Shakespeare, All's Well That Ends Well

"Love all" promotes a compassionate, sympathetic, and understanding attitude toward others. It serves as a reminder of the importance of treating everyone with love and respect, regardless of their background, beliefs, or differences. "Trust a few" is realistic and cautionary. While it is admirable to approach others with an open heart, the quote urges us to be cautious when putting our faith in others. "Do no wrong to none" is a moral imperative emphasizing the need of treating others fairly and ethically. It embodies the idea of exercising kindness, justice, and respect by emphasizing the principle of treating others as we would like to be treated.

July 30th

"If you can dream it, you can do it." – Walt Disney

Dreams are the seeds of change, growth, and innovation. They represent our deepest wants and goals, which frequently surpass our existing circumstances. The ability to imagine and see can lead to real-world accomplishments.

July 31st

"A bad day doesn't cancel out a good life. Keep going."
– Richie Norton

Life is full of ups and downs, and everyone encounters moments of difficulty or irritation. This quote reminds us that while we may have difficult days, they do not define our entire life. Let's avoid exaggerating the significance of a single poor day and instead concentrate on the big picture.

August 1st

"It is not that we have a short time to live, but that we waist a lot of it. Life is long enough, and a sufficient generous amount has been given to us for the highest achievements if it were all well invested. But when it is wasted in heedless luxury and spent on no good activity, we are forced at last by death's final constraint to realize that it has passed away before we know it was passing" – Seneca

The true issue is not how long we live, but how we use the time we have been given. A life spent on temporary pleasures or meaningless distractions eventually leads to regret. The quote encourages us to change our focus to activities that actually matter and connect with our ideals by drawing attention to the reality of mortality.

August 2nd

"I'm really very self-confident when it comes to my work. When I take on a project, I believe in it 100%. I really put my soul into it. I'd die for it. That's how I am." – Michael Jackson

This mindset is frequently associated with those who are driven by a strong sense of purpose and a desire to make a significant influence through their work. It demonstrates a level of dedication that can lead to extraordinary results, since the person's unwavering belief and dedication can be the driving force behind their accomplishments.

August 3rd

"You can't give up! If you give up, you're like everybody else."
– Chris Evert

Giving up is the same as accepting mediocrity or the status quo. By refusing to give up, a person distinguishes themselves from the crowd and demonstrates a determination to overcome challenges and obstacles. Giving up is the easiest way out, and it is something that many people will do. Those that refuse to give up, on the other hand, are the ones who stand out and accomplish greatness.

August 4th

"Life without experience and sufferings is not life." – Socrates

It is a vital part of what it is to genuinely live to experience both the highs and lows of life, including hardships and obstacles. A life free of difficulties and setbacks may be lacking in depth and meaning. We typically uncover our strengths, ideals, and the genuine nature of our character when we face adversity.

August 5th

"If you don't build your dream, someone else will hire you to help them build theirs." -Tony Gaskins

If we do not aggressively pursue our dreams and goals, we may end up working to fulfill someone else's goal instead. Choosing to create and follow your own goal involves perseverance, hard effort, and a willingness to accept risks, but it also provides the opportunity for enormous satisfaction and a sense of purpose.

August 6th

"If you realize that all things change, there is nothing you will try to hold on to." – Lao Tzu

When we completely understand and accept that everything in life is subject to change – whether it's situations, relationships, emotions, or material goods – we are free of the weight of clinging to the past or worrying about the future. The source of our suffering is typically our attachment to things, people, or situations that will change or fade away. Recognizing life's impermanence encourages us to create a mindset of detachment and acceptance.

August 7th

"We have to continually be jumping off cliffs and developing our wings on the way down." – Kurt Vonnegut

The concept of "developing our wings on the way down" emphasizes the fact that we don't necessarily need to have everything sorted out before taking action. It is about accepting uncertainty and believing in our own resilience and resourcefulness. Instead of waiting for ideal conditions or complete assurance, we are encouraged to take that first step, knowing that we will learn and adjust as we go, much like a bird learning to fly.

August 8th

"Predicting rain doesn't count. Building arks does." – Warren Buffett

It is not enough to anticipate challenges or obstacles; what is actually important is how we respond to them. By "building arks," we symbolize the proactive efforts we take to protect ourselves and our goals from possible difficulties. The essentials to weathering life's storms and navigating through uncertainties are preparation and action.

August 9th

"No one would have crossed the ocean if he could have gotten off the ship in the storm." – Charles Kettering

Meaningful accomplishments frequently involve enduring problems and uncertainty rather than looking for an easy way out. Storms and obstacles are unavoidable components of any big goal, and ignoring them may result in the loss of key experiences and accomplishments. Great successes are frequently the result of a willingness to face setbacks and stay the course, even when the road ahead seems uncertain or challenging.

August 10th

"You never really understand a person until you consider things from his point of view. Until you climb inside of his skin and walk around in it." – Harper Lee, To Kill a Mockingbird

Gaining a deep understanding of another person requires us to temporarily adopt their point of view. This includes setting aside our own biases and preconceptions and becoming receptive to the world as they see it. We extend our horizons and create a more nuanced grasp of the human experience when we take the time to analyze things from someone else's perspective.

August 11th

"There are only two ways to live your life. One is as though nothing is a miracle. The other is as though everything is a miracle."
– Albert Einstein

Our perspective on the world has a significant impact on our emotions, attitudes, and interactions. Miracles can be found in the ordinary – a beautiful sunset, a child's laughter, or the delicate details of nature. By adopting this perspective, we open ourselves up to a deeper connection with the world and a greater appreciation for the richness of life.

August 12th

"Success seems to be connected with action. Successful people keep moving. They make mistakes but they don't quit." – Conrad Hilton

Those who persevere in the face of difficulties are more likely to achieve their objectives. This resilience arises from a strong commitment to their goals and refusal to give up no matter how difficult the journey.

August 13th

"In dreams and in love there are no impossibilities." – Janos Arany

Dreams are representations of our deepest wishes and aspirations. They provide a canvas on which what seemed impossible becomes possible, allowing us to explore opportunities beyond the limitations of reality. Similarly, the concept of defying chances and overcoming barriers is frequently associated with love. Love has the extraordinary potential to transform people, inspiring them to become better versions of themselves. Whether it's love between lovers, friends, family members, or even a passion for a cause, the intensity of genuine love can lead to acts and consequences that would otherwise be believed unachievable.

August 14th

"If you really look closely, most overnight successes took a long time."
– Steve Jobs

Do not become discouraged by comparing yourself to apparent overnight success stories. What appears to be a quick and easy ascension to success is usually the result of years of hard work, persistence, and learning. Many people who are promoted as "overnight successes" have been quietly working on their skills, taking risks, and pushing their boundaries for a long time.

August 15th

"I attribute my success to this: I never gave or took an excuse."
– Florence Nightingale

Excuses can frequently become impediments to success. They have the potential to hinder progress, reduce motivation, and limit future growth. Individuals set a high standard for themselves by adopting the idea of not making or accepting excuses. Taking charge of our actions and decisions is critical to attaining our goals and becoming the best versions of ourselves.

August 16th

"Let your plans be dark and impenetrable as night, and when you move, fall like a thunderbolt."– Sun Tzu, The Art of War

"Let your plans be as dark and impenetrable as night" emphasizes the importance of keeping one's intentions hidden from opponents or competitors. This does not imply deceit, but rather the capacity to strategically withhold information until the proper time. "When you move, fall like a thunderbolt," underlines the significance of quick and decisive action once the strategy is in motion. Executing a well-concealed strategy with speed and precision can have a tremendous impact, much like a thunderbolt that hits unexpectedly and with immense force.

August 17th

"Nothing is more honorable than a grateful heart." – Seneca

A grateful heart acknowledges and appreciates the kindness and blessings that come our way. The honor of a thankful heart is found not only in the act of expressing gratitude, but also in the way it forms our character and influences our interactions. It serves as a continual reminder that, no matter what, there is always something to be thankful for.

August 18th

"Don't be distracted by criticism. Remember—the only taste of success some people get is to take a bite out of you." – Zig Ziglar

Some people may seek validation or a sense of accomplishment by demeaning those who are progressing. This is an important reminder that your accomplishments and endeavors are your own, and they should not be lessened by the opinions of others.

August 19th

"When we strive to become better than we are, everything around us becomes better too." – Paulo Coelho

We engage in a process of self-awareness, learning, and development as we strive to be better versions of ourselves. This personal progress frequently entails overcoming obstacles, learning new abilities, and adopting a growth mindset. Our enhanced self-confidence and abilities radiate outward as we embark on this journey of self-improvement, influencing many aspects of our lives. Our efforts to improve ourselves do not live in isolation; they have a ripple effect on our surroundings, relationships, and experiences.

August 20th

"The greatest discovery of any generation is that a human can alter his life by altering his attitude." – William James

By changing our attitude, we begin a process of transformation that can extend to our actions, decisions, and encounters. This concept is very empowering since it implies that we have the potential to change our reality by choosing our responses to circumstances consciously.

August 21st

"Appear as you may wish to be" – Niccolò Machiavelli

We are more likely to exhibit confidence, competence, and positivity when we project these qualities in our activities and relationships. We can build a feedback loop that encourages our growth and development by embodying the traits we wish to have. We can determine not just how others see us, but also how we view ourselves and the path we pursue in our personal and professional life, by connecting our outer expression with our interior objectives.

August 22nd

"You have power over your mind – not outside events. Realize this, and you will find strength." – Marcus Aurelius

This perspective is empowering because it turns our focus from feeling helpless in the face of difficulties to recognizing that we have the ability to shape our own inner environment. When we fully understand the difference between external occurrences and our reactions to them, we improve our inner strength. True resilience comes from our power to choose how we interpret and respond to our surroundings.

August 23rd

"May you live every day of your life." – Jonathan Swift

Our time on Earth is limited so we should make the most of it by seeing each day as an opportunity for improvement, connection, and joy. "May you live" promotes active engagement in life rather than simple survival. It's a reminder to be present, to live, to learn, and to grow.

August 24th

"You put your intention and your attention on what it is that you want to shift and change." – Wayne Dyer

We build a synergy that propels us toward transformation by aligning our intention (our desired outcome) with our attention (our concentrated efforts). Change does not happen by accident; it requires a purposeful effort to align our intentions and attention. By doing so, we empower ourselves to implement the desired adjustments and changes, resulting in personal growth and fulfillment.

August 25th

"Appear weak when you are strong, and strong when you are weak."
– Sun Tzu, The Art of War

It should be noted that this quote does not encourage lying or manipulation for negative objectives. Instead, it implies that there may be a tactical advantage in altering how people perceive us depending on the circumstances. Individuals that use strategic perception may be able to overcome challenges, achieve their goals, and keep an element of surprise.

August 26th

"Integrity is doing the right thing, even when no one is watching."
– C.S. Lewis

Integrity is based on conforming to one's moral and ethical ideals consistently, regardless of external conditions. It demonstrates a dedication to doing what is right and principled, even when there is no immediate accountability. When faced with temptations, shortcuts, or an opportunity to gain personal benefit, practicing integrity might require determination and strength. Integrity plays an essential role in shaping one's character and sense of self. It promotes personal development, self-esteem, and a strong sense of identity.

August 27th

"Above all things, respect yourself." – Pythagoras

Individuals who respect themselves prioritize their own well-being. This encompasses looking after one's physical, emotional, and mental health, as well as fostering their personal growth and development. It is fundamental to respect yourself by creating appropriate boundaries and living truthfully. Individuals who prioritize self-respect over everything else establish a positive sense of self while cultivating lives marked by confidence, empowerment, and meaningful connections.

August 28th

"You're under no obligation to be the same person you were 5 minutes ago." – Alan Watts

The quote encourages people to break free from the constraints of past actions, beliefs, or mistakes by stressing that there is no need to remain the same. It suggests that it is possible to break free from negative cycles and embrace beneficial developments. Every moment is a chance for self-improvement and regeneration.

August 29th

"I find that the harder I work, the more luck I seem to have."
– Thomas Jefferson

Individuals who work hard and persistently are more prepared to seize opportunities that come their way, which may appear to others as luck but is actually the consequence of their own determination. Consistent dedication and perseverance can lead to settings in which favorable outcomes are more likely. You can be responsible for your own luck.

August 30th

"The superior man is distressed by the limitations of his ability; he is not distressed by the fact that men do not recognize the ability that he has."
— Confucius

Instead than worrying about external validation, the superior individual concentrates on improving their skills, knowledge, and abilities. They focus their efforts on being the best version of themselves, regardless of whether others acknowledge.

August 31st

"Ordinary people merely think how they shall 'spend' their time; a man of talent tries to 'use' it."— Arthur Schopenhauer

People that have talent are proactive and intentional in their actions. Rather than allowing time to slip away, they make conscious decisions about how they allocate their time to tasks and activities that correspond with their goals and contribute to personal growth or achievement. Those who have talent recognize the importance of each moment. They seek to maximize their time by using it to learn, create, and achieve. This mindset motivates people to make thoughtful judgments and prioritize tasks that lead to advancement.

September 1st

"Take up one idea. Make that one idea your life — think of it, dream of it, live on that idea. Let the brain, muscles, nerves, every part of your body be full of that idea, and just leave every other idea alone. This is the way to success." — Swami Vivekananda

The quote emphasizes the importance of passion and perseverance. When a person is sincerely committed to their chosen idea, they are more likely to endure in the face of obstacles and disappointments, eventually reaching success. Unwavering commitment to an idea, combined with strong action, can result in amazing achievements and fulfillment in life.

September 2nd

"The human mind is our fundamental resource." – *John F. Kennedy*

From the depths of human thinking and imagination, there are limitless opportunities for discovery, exploration, and success. The mind is a never-ending source of growth and development. Education, curiosity, and intellectual interests can all lead to personal and community enrichment.

September 3rd

"I learned to always take on things I'd never done before. Growth and comfort do not coexist." – *Virginia Rometty*

We open ourselves up to growth, learning, and self-improvement by stepping into unfamiliar territory and taking on things that are outside of our comfort zone. True success is the result of a determination to embrace discomfort and push ourselves beyond our limits. We boost our chances of accomplishing our objectives and desires by constantly seeking growth and progress.

September 4th

"Life is a journey, not a destination." – *Ralph Waldo Emerson*

Rather than focusing simply on future goals or outcomes, what matters most is the process of living and experiencing life. The quote inspires us to appreciate the numerous stages, obstacles, and experiences we face along the road by viewing life as a journey. It inspires us to find purpose and fulfillment in the activities and interactions that shape our lives on a daily basis.

September 5th

"Morality is not the doctrine of how we may make ourselves happy, but of how we may make ourselves worthy of happiness." – Immanuel Kant

Morality's real purpose is to guide humans toward acts and choices that are consistent with values, virtues, and ethical principles. In this setting, morality is deeply linked to characteristics such as honesty, compassion, fairness, and empathy. Through adopting these characteristics, people lay the groundwork for a more significant and fulfilled existence.

September 6th

"Things work out best for those who make the best of how things work out." – John Wooden

Those who approach life with positivity and resilience are more likely to achieve successful results, even when conditions aren't quite ideal. We must adjust our perspective and make the best of the situation at hand rather than fixate on outcomes that may not meet our expectations.

September 7th

"Don't take things too personally. Critique, failures, unwarranted advice – take it to mind, not to heart. What you hear out of the mouths of others are opinions and perspectives. It's often worth listening to opinions and perspectives, but it's not a requisite that you take them on board." – Nate Hamon

It is critical to cultivate emotional resilience by not taking things personally. Even in the face of criticism or failure, it is essential to maintain a balanced and healthy emotional state. By advising us to "take it to mind, not to heart," the quote encourages the concept of establishing healthy boundaries between external input and our own self-worth.

September 8th

"Change your thoughts and you change your world."
– Norman Vincent Peale

We may change our sense of reality and, as a result, our interactions with the world by modifying our thought patterns. We must pay great attention to our mindsets and address any negative or restricting thoughts that may be preventing us from moving forward.

September 9th

"Success is the product of daily habits – not once in a lifetime transformation. – James Clear

Success is not dependent on short bursts of effort, but on the constant behaviors we engage in through our lives. It is about establishing a foundation of habits that can be sustained over time, leading to long-term success.

September 10th

"Keep away from people who try to belittle your ambitions. Small people always do that, but the really great make you feel that you, too, can become great." – Mark Twain

Small-minded people may try to diminish our goals, perhaps because they are constrained by their own limits. Their skepticism and criticism, however, should not stop us. The genuinely amazing people, those who have achieved greatness themselves, are the ones who recognize possibility in us. Their encouragement and support act as a motivator, urging us to aim higher and reach farther. So, let us turn away from the critics and join those who boost us up. Let us pick the path of empowerment, becoming inspired and inspiring others.

September 11th

"I believe that if you think small, you'll stay small."
— Ray Kroc, Grinding It Out: The Making of McDonald's

A limited or restrictive mentality may hinder progress. Individuals can be held back from realizing their full potential by self-imposed constraints and negative ideas. When we trust in our own potential for excellence, we are more willing to take bold steps toward realizing it.

September 12th

"When I was 5 years old, my mother always told me that happiness was the key to life. When I went to school, they asked me what I wanted to be when I grew up. I wrote down 'happy'. They told me I didn't understand the assignment, and I told them they didn't understand life." — John Lennon

Let's put happiness first and make sure that our lives are lived with authenticity, passion, and purpose. By realizing that happiness is a state of being rather than a destination, we can find contentment along the way and transform life into a joyful journey.

September 13th

"The real test is not whether you avoid this failure, because you won't. It's whether you let it harden or shame you into inaction, or whether you learn from it; whether you choose to persevere."
— Barack Obama

Failure is not the end, but rather an essential component of the journey. The true measure of character is not whether you stumble, but whether you rise above it, learn from your mistakes, and continue to strive for greatness.

September 14th

"If you set your goals ridiculously high and it's a failure, you will fail above everyone else's success." – James Cameron

Even if our ambitious goals result in momentary setbacks or disappointments, the act of striving for greatness propels us far above mediocrity. Failure in the pursuit of audacious goals indicate that we are not afraid to take chances and strive for the extraordinary. When we dare to dream big and work tirelessly to achieve our goals, our failures become stepping stones on a less traveled path that leads us to a level of achievement that few have ventured to imagine.

September 15th

"Absorb what is useful, discard what is not, add what is uniquely your own." – Bruce Lee

To "absorb what is useful" means to be a lifelong learner who is open to new information and experiences."Discarding what is not" is a focus and efficiency exercise. It helps us to clear out the clutter and distractions that are holding us back, leaving mental and emotional space available for what really is important. "Adding what is uniquely your own" refers to combining the lessons, insights, and inspirations we've gathered into something new and authentic.

September 16th

"A man sees in the world what he carries in his heart."
– Johann Wolfgang von Goethe

We are more prone to see the world through a pessimistic lens if we hold negativity, resentment, or cynicism within us. If our hearts are filled with positivity, love, and joy, we are more likely to notice the world's beauty, opportunities, and kindness.

September 17th

"Men are driven by two principal impulses, either by love or by fear."
– Niccolò Machiavelli, Discourses

Are your decisions motivated by love, by a real desire to create and connect? Or are you responding out of fear, allowing our anxieties and concerns to drive our decisions?

September 18th

"No amount of anxiety makes any difference to anything that is going to happen." – Alan Watts

We waste precious energy worrying about what-ifs and worstcase situations, only to discover that these concerns have no effect on the outcomes we confront. Instead of concentrating on our worries we can concentrate on what we can control: our attitudes, behaviors, and efforts. Recognizing that worry has no control over external situations empowers us to handle life's twists and turns more successfully.

September 19th

"Success is no accident. It is hard work, perseverance, learning, studying, sacrifice and most of all, love of what you are doing or learning to do." – Pelé

Every accomplishment is built with hard work. Sweat and hustle, long hours, and a relentless quest for excellence pave the route for success. The refusal to give up, especially in the face of difficulties, distinguishes those who succeed from those who fail.

September 20th

"In the long run, the sharpest weapon of all is a kind and gentle spirit."
– Anne Frank

A kind and gentle spirit has the ability to disarm even the hardest hearts and alleviate difficult circumstances. It is not a sign of weakness, but rather of inner strength and knowledge.

September 21st

"You're braver than you believe, and stronger than you seem, and smarter than you think." – A.A. Milne

We have an inclination to underestimate ourselves, failing to recognize our own potential. Believing in ourselves is the foundation for personal growth and achievement. We are prone to pursue our objectives and goals with dedication and passion when we understand our own worth and potential.

September 22nd

"Successful people do what unsuccessful people are not willing to do. Don't wish it were easier; wish you were better." – Jim Rohn

Successful people are willing to put in the time, effort, and dedication that others tend to avoid. They recognize that pushing through difficulties, stepping out of comfort zones, and continually opting for choices that line with their goals are necessary for growth and achievement. The advice to "wish you were better" in the quote is a call to self-improvement. Instead of waiting for things to change or looking for shortcuts, the emphasis is on personal development and becoming better prepared to face obstacles.

September 23rd

"The secret of change is to focus all of your energy not on fighting the old, but on building the new." – Socrates

Change is not about concentrating on what must be left behind; it is about building something new and better. When we focus our efforts on developing new habits, skills, and strategies, we generate momentum that propels us ahead. We can direct our efforts toward something that has the potential to bring us growth, improvement, and fulfillment.

September 24th

"Courage doesn't always roar. Sometimes courage is the little voice at the end of the day that says I'll try again tomorrow."
– Mary Anne Radmacher

Courage can be a constant flame that burns within us. It isn't always glamorous or loud, but it is steady and resilient. It is the courage to recognize our limitations, to embrace failure as a necessary part of growth, and to find hope even in the face of challenges.

September 25th

"Bad things are not the worst thing that can happen to us. Nothing is the worst thing that can happen to us." – Richard Bach

We often fear bad outcomes or difficult situations, but this quote encourages us to consider something far more important to be concerned about: a condition of nothingness, a lack of growth, experience, or advancement. The true danger is stagnation, not taking risks, and not pursuing our interests and aspirations. We miss out on life's opportunities for growth, learning, and transformation when we allow ourselves to stay stuck in a condition of inertia.

September 26th

"Stay close to anything that makes you glad you are alive." – Hafez

Our sources of joy can take various forms, including spending quality time with loved ones, engaging in creative activities, appreciating nature's beauty, pursuing important goals, and simply savoring the small moments of everyday life. We create a sense of appreciation and contentment when we prioritize and spend our time and energy in these pleasant experiences, which can have a tremendous impact on our attitude on life.

September 27th

"Every child is an artist. The problem is how to remain an artist once he grows up." – Pablo Picasso

As we become older, societal expectations, self-doubt, and daily life duties can hinder our creative urges. We may begin to value practicality over passion, conformity over originality, and predictability over taking risks. The task, then, is to uncover and embrace our artistic essence rather than just preserve and protect it.

September 28th

"Luck? I don't know anything about luck. I've never banked on it and I'm afraid of people who do. Luck to me is something else: Hard work – and realizing what is an opportunity and what isn't."
– Lucille Ball

"Luck" in her eyes is directly related to our ability to recognize opportunities for advancement. It is about being aware of our environment, remaining open to new experiences, and having the confidence to take calculated risks. In essence, luck is the ability to recognize opportunity and act on it.

September 29th

"One can live magnificently in this world if one knows how to work and how to love. – Leo Tolstoy

When we find work that connects with our inner selves, it stops being an obligation and becomes a source of inspiration and joy. It gives us the ability to engage, learn, and grow, resulting in a sense of accomplishment and happiness. Love plays an equally vital function in our lives. It includes not only romantic love, but also love for one's family, friends, community, and even ourselves. By cultivating our potential for meaningful work and sincere love, we may create a life that is not only prosperous, but also gratifying and full of meaning.

September 30th

"Some people look for a beautiful place. Others make a place beautiful."
– Hazrat Inayat Khan

Ordinary environments can be transformed into remarkable ones by our actions and attitudes. Instead of simply seeking beauty, let us take the effort to become creators of our environment, transforming it into a place that reflects joy, warmth, and inspiration.

October 1st

"If you are not willing to risk the usual, you will have to settle for the ordinary." – Jim Rohn

The road to spectacular achievements is not paved with the mundane and familiar. Don't settle for average when you have the potential to accomplish something genuinely extraordinary. The usual may be comfortable, but the extraordinary is where your true potential awaits.

October 2nd

"Do not be afraid of tasting the bitterness of failure. Be brave. The sweetness of success will before long befriend you. – Sri Chinmoy

Accepting the bitterness of failure is like planting the seeds of future success. Just as a seed buried in soil requires time, patience, and nurturing to grow into a flourishing plant, your experiences, even the painful ones, are necessary components of your path to success.

October 3rd

"The most courageous act is still to think for yourself. Aloud."
– Coco Chanel

Those who dare to express their own thoughts and ideas are the most courageous people. When you express your true self, you are not only embracing your individuality, but you are also laying the path for change and growth.

October 4th

"When one door closes, another opens; but we often look so long and so regretfully upon the closed door that we do not see the one that has opened for us." – Alexander Graham Bell

We risk missing out on numerous opportunities, adventures, and experiences that await us if we focus on closed doors. Every closed door presents the possibility of further development, learning, and the discovery of something even better. Let go of your regrets, look ahead with optimism, and be ready to go through the open doors that await you.

October 5th

"You become what you give your attention to. If you do not choose what thoughts and images you expose yourself to, someone else will."
– Epictetus

It's easy to allow outside forces to influence us. But we must choose to exert control over our own mental environment. We are in charge of the thoughts we entertain, the information we absorb, and the visuals we see. Our inner environment has a direct influence on our external experiences. If we continually dwell on negativity or allow unproductive ideas to overtake us, we may find ourselves deviating from the path we desire. We must be cautious about what we allow into our minds. We have the power to construct our own reality through the thoughts we nurture.

October 6th

"The best remedy for anger is delay." – Seneca

Reacting impulsively to anger can often result in regrettable acts or words. Taking a step back to collect our thoughts and allow the initial wave of anger to pass can lead to more conscious and constructive responses. We allow ourselves the opportunity to gain perspective on the situation, contemplate the potential ramifications of our actions, and choose a solution that is more compatible with our values and goals by postponing our reaction.

October 7th

"Never give up on a dream just because of the time it will take to accomplish it. The time will pass anyway." – Earl Nightingale

Time is a constant in our life, and whether we use it to follow our goals or not, it will continue to pass. So why not devote that time to something that is actually meaningful to us? The road to our dreams may be long, but each step we take brings us closer to our destination.

October 8th

"The limit is not the sky. The limit is your mind." – Wim Hof

The main barrier to our success and growth is frequently our own mind. We can push beyond imagined limits and achieve things that once seemed impossible by broadening our mentality and believing in our own skills. The quote encourages us to dream large, establish daring goals, and pursue them fiercely. It's a call to break free from our own limitations and strive for the remarkable.

October 9th

"He who suffers before it is necessary, suffers more than is necessary"
– Seneca

Our fears and anxiety about the future can increase our pain beyond what is necessary. By suffering in advance over imagined scenarios, we deprive ourselves of the joy and contentment of the current moment. It is critical to address challenges when they arise, rather than allowing anxiety and anticipation to increase our suffering.

October 10th

"The scariest moment is always just before you start." – Stephen King

The thought of starting something new or stepping outside of your comfort zone can be terrifying. But keep in mind that it's during those moments of anxiety and uncertainty that you're on the verge of something incredible. That initial fear, like the initial ascend on a rollercoaster before the amazing drop, is an indicator that something incredible is about to happen. Consider all of your previous accomplishments. Were they not preceded by moments of apprehension? Accept your fear, understand it, and then take that brave step forward. Once you get past your initial fear, you'll learn you're more capable than you ever believed.

October 11th

"The price of anything is the amount of life you exchange for it."
– Henry David Thoreau

We must analyze the true cost of our decisions and determine whether they are in line with our interests and goals. Time is the most valuable resource we have, and every decision we make means exchanging a portion of our lives for something else. Let's focus on investing our time and energy purposefully in the things that genuinely matter to us, and being willing to let go of what is not compatible with our values or does not bring us fulfillment.

October 12th

"Chains of habit are too light to be felt until they are too heavy to be broken." – Warren Buffett

It's easy to underestimate the influence of little, consistent actions over time, but our habits gradually establish patterns that can either uplift us or hold us back. We must be careful of the habits we create; small actions add up and shape the direction of our life.

October 13th

"It's not the load that breaks you down, it's the way you carry it."
– Lena Horne

Life presents us with obstacles and burdens, but it is not the weight of these challenges that defines our fate, but how we choose to deal with them. Our attitude, mindset, and approach all have a huge impact on our experiences. Just like a properly adjusted and carried backpack feels lighter, the problems we confront become more manageable when we choose to meet them with a positive attitude and a determined spirit.

October 14th

"If you want to live a happy life, tie it to a goal, not to people or things."– Albert Einstein

When we tie our happiness to people or things, we risk having our emotions influenced by external variables over which we have no control. When we connect our happiness to our goals, on the other hand, we obtain a sense of control and fulfillment. Goals provide us a feeling of purpose, something to strive for, and a road map for personal development. Setting and achieving important goals enables us to shape our own happiness, independent of external circumstances.

October 15th

"Don't chase people. Be yourself, do your own thing and work hard. The right people – the ones who really belong in your life – will come to you. And stay. – Will Smith

Pursuing others or attempting to fit into someone else's mold can be draining and unsatisfying. Instead, when we focus on our own development and happiness, we attract people who share our beliefs and objectives. Continue to be yourself, to work hard, and to live your truth. The right people will find their way to you.

October 16th

"Happiness is when what you think, what you say, and what you do are in harmony." – Mahatma Gandhi

When our inner thoughts align with the words we say and the acts we conduct, we create a harmonious and authentic life that is truly fulfilling. Striving for this balance involves self-awareness and purposeful choices. This quote motivates us to examine our values, thoughts, and behaviors and, if necessary, make changes.

October 17th

"You are what you think. So just think big, believe big, act big, work big, give big, forgive big, laugh big, love big and live big."
– Andrew Carnegie

Your thoughts are the seeds of your reality, and thinking big sets the stage for huge accomplishments. Believing in your abilities, acting confidently, and putting in the work will pave the road for extraordinary achievements.

October 18th

"Courage is not the absence of fear, but rather the assessment that something else is more important than fear." – Franklin D. Roosevelt

When fear creeps in, understand that it is a normal part of the journey. But keep in mind that your ambitions, potential, and the impact you can make are far more important than any fear that may be holding you back. Allow your courage to guide you, and you'll find yourself accomplishing things you never imagined possible. Your dreams are far more valuable than your fears.

October 19th

"Another person cannot hurt you without your cooperation; you are hurt the moment you believe yourself to be." – Epictetus

We regain our power when we absorb the idea that we have a choice in how we respond to outside influences. We realize that no one can actually harm us without our permission. Pain is caused not by the actions of others, but by our interpretations and beliefs about those behaviors. You preserve your own happiness by choosing to rise above harmful situations and emotions.

October 20th

"Comparison is the thief of joy." – Theodore Roosevelt

It's tempting to compare our journey, accomplishments, and circumstances to those of others, and in doing so, we deprive ourselves of the real satisfaction that comes from enjoying our own unique path. Each of us is on our own journey, with our own set of strengths, flaws, obstacles, and triumphs. Accepting this truth frees us from the suffocating hold of comparison, allowing us to create genuine contentment from within.

October 21st

"Well done is better than well said." – Benjamin Franklin

Our acts are more powerful than our words. While discussing our objectives and desires is important, it is the actions we take to make those words a reality that truly matter. It's simple to make promises and talk about our goals, but the true impact is achieved when we take significant actions toward them.

October 22nd

"What worries you masters you." – John Locke

Worries may easily affect our actions, decisions, and overall well-being when we allow them to dominate our minds. Imagine the freedom that comes from realizing that worrying is a choice and that we can regain control of our lives by taking control of our thoughts. This is your reminder to be present in the moment, to face issues with a clear mind, and to take proactive measures to find solutions rather than drowning in worries.

October 23rd

"Always work hard on something uncomfortably exciting!"
– Larry E. Page

Embrace the discomfort, appreciate the excitement, and direct your efforts toward something that makes your heart beat faster. Continue pushing, working hard, and pursuing those fascinating endeavors that will transform you into the great person you are meant to be!

October 24th

"Our anxiety does not come from thinking about the future, but from wanting to control it." *– Khalil Gibran*

Rather than attempting to control every aspect of the future, we can focus on the current moment and take proactive efforts while acknowledging that we cannot control everything. We can release the weight of anxiety by letting go of our desire for excessive control and adopting a more open and adaptable approach.

October 25th

"Time can be an ally or an enemy. What it becomes depends entirely upon you, your goals, and your determination to use every available minute." *– Zig Ziglar*

Make mindful decisions to devote time to activities that are in line with your goals. Take advantage of every opportunity, optimize your efforts, and allow time to be your dedicated partner in accomplishing the remarkable. Your journey is in your control, and if you work hard enough, time will become your most important asset on the way to success.

October 26th

"Each day that you're moving toward your dreams without compromising who you are, you're winning." – Michael Dell

Progress is not only about the destination; it is also about the journey and the decisions you make along the way. Your route to success is entirely unique to you, and each day you remain devoted to your principles and objectives, you triumph over obstacles and setbacks.

October 27th

"We know what we are, but know not what we may be."
– William Shakespeare, Hamlet

Believe in your ability to achieve greatness. Your story is still being written, and you have the chance to mold and redefine yourself with each chapter. So keep moving forward with confidence, for the future is full with opportunity to find and release your true potential.

October 28th

"More is lost by indecision than wrong decision."
– Marcus Tullius Cicero

Indecision can imprison us in a loop of uncertainty and keep us from progressing. When we hesitate to make a decision, we are ultimately wasting valuable time that could have been spent exploring new possibilities, learning from mistakes, and growing as individuals. Accepting that mistakes are only stepping stones to growth and learning can empower us to take risks and make confident choices. Remember that even if a decision does not result in the anticipated goal, the experience acquired can be extremely beneficial for future initiatives.

October 29th

"How much time one saves who does not look to see what their neighbor says or does or thinks." – Marcus Aurelius

Too much focus on the opinions and behaviors of others can be a significant drain on our time and energy. When we constantly compare ourselves to others, we waste precious time that could be spent following our own passions, dreams, and goals. The path to self-discovery and success is found within

October 30th

"When setting out on a journey do not seek advice from those who have never left home." – Rumi

It is not a matter of dismissing well-intended advice from others, but rather of determining whose counsel aligns with your objectives and desires. Surrounding yourself with those who have taken risks may be a source of inspiration and empowerment, helping you toward your own discoveries, growth, and transformation.

October 31st

"There is no royal road to a successful life, as there is no royal road to learning. It has got to be hard knocks, morning, noon, and night, and fixity of purpose." – Charles M. Schwab

There is no magical shortcut to living a full and successful life, just as there is no shortcut to acquiring knowledge. Success is not for the faint of heart, but for those who are willing to put in the effort, learn from their mistakes, and stay focused on their goals.

November 1st

"You can easily judge the character of a man by how he treats those who can do nothing for him" – Johann Von Goethe

Respecting everyone, regardless of social status or perceived usefulness, exhibits integrity and empathy. True character is defined not just by how we appear in public, but also by how we constantly act when no one is looking. So, regardless of their status or influence, let us strive to treat everyone with compassion and respect, because it is in these moments that our true character is shown.

November 2nd

"The best way to not feel hopeless is to get up and do something. Don't wait for good things to happen to you. If you go out and make some good things happen, you will fill the world with hope, you will fill yourself with hope." – Barack Obama

The key that unlocks the door to hope is action. When we take initiative and work for our objectives, we not only change our surroundings, but we also build a sense of purpose and persistence within ourselves. We take charge of our destiny and pave the way for hope to grow by refusing to wait for good things to come our way.

November 3rd

"I've had a lot of worries in my life, most of which never happened."
– Mark Twain

The human mind has a tendency to imagine situations that may never come true, producing unnecessary tension and anxiety. So, when faced with worries, keep in mind that many of them might never actually happen. This awareness can help you approach difficulties with a more balanced mentality, concentrating on solutions rather than the what-ifs.

November 4th

"Failure is simply the opportunity to begin again, this time more intelligently." – Henry Ford

Don't let a wrong move define you. Use it to improve your strategy, learn important lessons, and keep moving forward. Failure is not the end, but rather an opportunity to rewrite your story with more knowledge and determination.

November 5th

"Intelligence without ambition is a bird without wings." – Salvador Dali

Intelligence provides the tools and knowledge, while ambition propels you to take flight and do extraordinary things. It's not only about having the ability; it's about having the motivation to turn that skill into actual results. Your ambitions provide direction and purpose to your intelligence, just as a bird requires its wings to soar to great heights. They energize your efforts, direct your behaviors, and push you outside of your comfort zone. So, let intelligence serve as the foundation and ambition serve as the wind beneath your wings.

November 6th

"Emancipate yourselves from mental slavery, none but ourselves can free our minds." – Bob Marley

We have the potential to free our brains from the doubts, fears, and constraints that limit us. Just like physical chains can be broken, so can the chains of negative thoughts and self-doubt. We must assume responsibility for our thoughts and beliefs, acknowledging our ability to construct our own perspectives.

November 7th

"It's strange how simple things become, once you see them clearly."
– Ayn Rand

Overthinking and complicating things can cloud our judgment, however obtaining clarity can reveal the path ahead. Stepping back, reevaluating, and seeking simplicity in our approach has significant benefits. We can focus on the essentials, prioritize what genuinely matters, and overcome problems with greater efficiency and effectiveness when we see things clearly.

November 8th

"It is important to remember that there are no overnight successes. You will need to be dedicated, single-minded, and there is no substitute to hard work." – Mukesh Ambani

Remember that great accomplishments are the product of constant effort, learning from mistakes, and pushing yourself outside of your comfort zone. So, keep your eyes on the prize and understand that while success may not always be quick or evident, it is the journey itself that shapes you into the person capable of greatness.

November 9th

"No one that encounters prosperity does not also encounter danger."
– Heraclitus

The rewards of endurance and dedication shine brightly in the face of adversity, just as the sun rises after the darkest night. You should never let the presence of danger or difficulty discourage you from pursuing your dreams. Remember that those who courageously face dangers on the path to success are the ones who emerge victorious, not just in their accomplishments, but also in the strength of character they've developed along the way.

November 10th

"Great minds discuss ideas; average minds discuss events; small minds discuss people." – Eleanor Roosevelt

Elevate your thinking and surround yourself with intelligent minds. Remember that your mindset is determined by your focus, so seek to be a part of conversations that uplift, inspire, and create positive outcomes.

November 11th

"Be impatient with action but patient with results." – Naval Ravikant

We remind ourselves to seize the moment, take decisive moves, and push our boundaries by being impatient with action. Embrace every opportunity to act with enthusiasm and commitment, but keep in mind that the fruits of your labor may take some time to fully develop.

November 12th

"If one only wished to be happy, this could be easily accomplished; but we wish to be happier than other people, and this is always difficult, for we believe others to be happier than they truly are." – Montesquieu

Our pursuit of happiness frequently involves comparisons with others, causing unnecessary difficulties. The truth is that happiness is a journey that is unique to each person. It is not a matter of being happier than others, but of finding happiness and joy in your own life. We unburden ourselves from the weight of comparison when we shift our focus from attempting to be "happier than others" to just pursuing happiness inside ourselves. We realize that appearances can be deceiving, and that everyone faces unique obstacles. Embracing our own journey allows us to embrace the small and big moments that actually bring us happiness.

November 13th

"There are two things a person should never be angry at, what they can help, and what they cannot." – Plato

Anger is an intense emotion that may obscure our judgment and drain our energy. Our strength derives in concentrating our efforts on things we can influence. It's a wake-up call to be proactive in making great changes in our life. When it comes to things beyond our control, though, accepting and understanding can lead to inner peace.

November 14th

"Courage is found in unlikely places." – J. R. R. Tolkien

Courage isn't just for the extraordinary; it's built into our everyday existence. It happens when we face uncertainty, make difficult decisions, and overcome setbacks. Remember, you are stronger than you believe, and courage may be discovered in the most unexpected places.

November 15th

"The future depends on what you do today." – Mahatma Gandhi

Embrace the power you have to shape your own destiny. Every small action you take, every goal you pursue, is a stepping stone toward the life you want. Allow today to serve as a reminder of your commitment to achieving the future you desire. Seize today's opportunities with passion and determination. Your current activities are the seeds that will blossom in the future.

November 16th

"There is no easy walk to freedom anywhere, and many of us will have to pass through the valley of the shadow of death again and again before we reach the mountaintop of our desires."
– Nelson Mandela

Remember that the greatest rewarding successes come from overcoming the most difficult challenges. So, when you find yourself in the valley of difficulties, remember to keep your focus on the mountaintop of your dreams. While you continue your ascension, remember that the summit of your desires is a symbol of your constant dedication and the wonderful adventure that led you there.

November 17th

"The wisest people follow their own direction." – Euripides

The route to wisdom is found in trusting your instincts and following your own unique path. While it is essential to learn from others and gain insights, you are the ultimate compass for your life's journey. Remember that it is okay to deviate from the standards and develop your own narrative. Each step you take towards your own direction is a step closer to living a life that is authentically yours.

November 18th

"Take a chance. It's the best way to test yourself. Have fun and push your boundaries." – Richard Branson

Don't be scared to try something new, to take on a difficult endeavor, or to pursue a dream that appears out of reach. Take a chance, enjoy the thrill of the unknown, and have fun along the way.

November 19th

"People do not decide their futures, they decide their habits and their habits decide their futures." – Frederick M. Alexander

We may lay a solid foundation for success by embracing beneficial habits. Whether it's practicing discipline, nourishing creativity, cultivating relationships, or maintaining a healthy lifestyle, these little, regular efforts add up to provide major results over time. The trick is to be intentional in the habits we choose to establish.

November 20th

"The future has several names. For the weak, it is impossible; for the fainthearted, it is unknown; but for the valiant, it is ideal."
– Victor Hugo

We have a choice in how we view our future, and our perspective has a significant impact on the outcomes we accomplish. Adopting a courageous attitude opens us up to the possibilities of the future, paving the way for personal growth, success, and fulfillment.

November 21st

"I am who I am today because of the choices I made yesterday."
– Eleanor Roosevelt

Every decision we make, no matter how minor, has an impact on our character, skills, and direction. It is critical to reflect on our previous decisions, learn from them, and apply what we have learned to make even better selections in the future.

November 22nd

"When you arise in the morning think of what a privilege it is to be alive, to think, to enjoy, to love…" – Marcus Aurelius

Starting the day with this perspective can be significantly transforming. It pushes us to shift our focus from the routine to the extraordinary, from the normal to the miraculous. We infuse purpose and joy into our acts by acknowledging the gift of life and the abilities we possess.

November 23rd

"Never give up. Today is hard, tomorrow will be worse, but the day after tomorrow will be sunshine." – Jack Ma

The concept of "sunshine after the storm" teaches us to be patient and resilient in the face of adversity. It reminds us that difficult times are just temporary and that perseverance will lead us to greater strength and success. So, if you are encountering difficulties, remember that every step you take today contributes to the happier days that await you in the future.

November 24th

"The ones who are crazy enough to think that they can change the world, are the ones who do." – Steve Jobs

The first step toward making your dreams a reality is to believe in your ability to make a difference. Accept your "crazy" ideas and allow them to drive your actions. Remember that every big change started with someone who believed they could make a difference – and in many cases, they were right.

November 25th

"Treat yourself like someone you're responsible for helping."
– Jordan Peterson

Treat yourself with the same level of care and attention you would give to a close friend or family member. This mindset helps you to prioritize self-care, set appropriate boundaries, and make decisions that benefit your physical, mental, and emotional health. It's about accepting that you deserve the same amount of love and attention that you give to others. Remember that you are responsible for your own well-being. Nurturing your physical, mental, and emotional health is not only an act of self-love, but it is also a requirement to live a good life.

November 26th

"Wherever you go, go with all your heart." – Confucius

Whether you're beginning a new chapter, pursuing a dream, or simply going about your everyday business, bring your heart along. It's not just about being physically present; it's about bringing true passion and dedication to every moment.

November 27th

"To a great mind, nothing is little." – Arthur Conan Doyle

We can live a fuller and more meaningful life if we recognize the significance of every detail. If you embrace each moment with openness and enthusiasm, you'll discover that the world is full of hidden treasures just waiting to be discovered.

November 28th

"Many people lose the small joys in the hope for the big happiness."
– Pearl S. Buck

We often overlook the beauty that can be found in the simple pleasures of everyday life in our pursuit of spectacular achievements or ultimate happiness. Embracing the small joys doesn't mean settling for less; it is about recognizing the worth of each moment and finding enjoyment in the present. So appreciate the little things – a warm cup of coffee, a peaceful sunset, laughter shared with friends – and find gratitude in the everyday moments.

November 29th

"Someone is sitting in the shade today because someone planted a tree a long time ago." – Warren Buffett

Even if our efforts appear small at the time, they can result in great advantages in the future. Just as it takes time for a tree to grow and offer shade, our activities may not produce immediate consequences. They can, however, build the groundwork for a brighter and more comfortable tomorrow.

November 30th

"You may encounter many defeats, but you must not be defeated. In fact, it may be necessary to encounter the defeats so you can know who you are, what you can rise from, how you can still come out of it."
– Maya Angelou

Embrace challenges because they will shape you into the person you are destined to be. Move forward with faith in your abilities to overcome any hurdle, and you will reach incredible heights.

December 1st

"Success isn't always about greatness. It's about consistency. Consistent hard work leads to success. Greatness will come." – Dwayne Johnson

Success isn't only about attaining greatness in one magnificent moment; it's about the daily grind, incremental progress, and steadfast dedication to your goals. Consistency is like a continuous drop of water carving out a canyon. The accumulation of effort day after day, leads to extraordinary achievements. Success is a marathon, not a sprint, and your perseverance will be your best ally on this journey.

December 2nd

"It is the nature of the wise to resist pleasures, but the foolish to be a slave to them." – Epictetus

In a world full of temptations and distractions, the wise recognize the significance of denying immediate pleasures in order to achieve higher, long-term goals. When we choose delayed satisfaction over rapid gratification, we enhance our character and establish the groundwork for a more fulfilling and purposeful existence. It's about realizing that true happiness typically comes from accomplishing meaningful objectives rather than quick pleasures.

December 3rd

"Whenever you see a successful person, you only see the public glories, never the private sacrifices to reach them." – Vaibhav Shah

Success is frequently the product of long hours of behindthe-scenes hard work, determination, and sacrifice. Every successful individual started as a beginner, endured failures, and overcame hurdles. But they persisted, learned from their mistakes, and kept going. Use their journey as inspiration for your own, knowing that with hard work and perseverance, you, too, can attain your goals and dreams.

December 4th

"Do not go where the path may lead, go instead where there is no path and leave a trail." – Ralph Waldo Emerson

Don't be scared to venture off the traditional path; it's in those uncharted territories that you may discover your greatest accomplishments and make an unforgettable impact on the world.

December 5th

"Don't wait around for other people to be happy for you. Any happiness you get you've got to make yourself." – Alice Walker

Our happiness does not rely on the approval or affirmation of others. It is an interior state of being that we have the ability to generate and nurture. We have control over our emotions and well-being, and we possess the potential to brighten each day with our own actions and mentality. So make your own happiness and allow it to radiate from within, inspiring everyone around you to do the same. Every day, you can offer yourself the gift of happiness.

December 6th

"One day you will wake up and there won't be any more time to do the thing you've always wanted. Do it now." – Paulo Coelho

If you want to do something, don't wait for the "perfect" moment because it may never arrive. Seize the day, act, and follow your dreams right now. Don't let fear or procrastination hold you back. Accept the present moment and start working toward your goals and passions. Remember that the best moment to begin is always right now.

December 7th

"You cannot hope to make progress in areas where you have taken no action." – Epictetus

Even if progress appears to be slow, each step forward is a step in the right direction. So, don't be scared to take action, no matter how small it may appear. Your efforts will add up over time, and you'll find yourself making great progress toward your goals.

December 8th

"Throughout life people will make you mad, disrespect you and treat you bad. Let God deal with the things they do, cause hate in your heart will consume you too." – Will Smith

Holding onto anger, resentment, or hate can be extremely harmful to your well-being. It's a burden that holds you back from enjoying true happiness and peacefulness within. Instead of focusing on the negative behaviors of others, it is healthier to concentrate on your own personal development and the positive aspects of your life. Choosing peace over holding grudges can be a freeing experience. It does not imply accepting or justifying harmful behavior, but rather liberating yourself from the emotional chains that can harm you.

December 9th

"The mind is furnished with ideas by experience alone." – John Locke

Each experience, whether positive or difficult, brings you knowledge. So, open your arms to life's adventures and challenges. Seek out new experiences; they will help you grow, learn, and broaden your thinking, making you a more well-rounded and intelligent person.

December 10th

"What we are today comes from our thoughts of yesterday, and our present thoughts build our life of tomorrow. Our life is the creation of our mind." – Gautama Buddha

We must take control of our thoughts and concentrate on optimism, progress, and resilience. We pave the way for a brighter and more rewarding future when we cultivate a positive and forwardthinking mindset. Our thoughts are like seeds that, with the correct nurturing, can grow into amazing realities.

December 11th

"Success is not the key to happiness; happiness is the key to success. If you love what you are doing, you will be successful."
– Albert Schweitzer

Our search for success should be motivated by the happiness and enthusiasm we feel for what we do. When we sincerely love what we're engaged in, success is a natural outcome of our dedication and passion. It is critical that we change our focus away from external measures of success and toward fostering our interior well-being. When we prioritize our happiness, we unlock our full potential and attract success that aligns with our true selves.

December 12th

"The past has no power over the present moment." – Eckhart Tolle

The past is a chapter we've already read, and it does not determine the story we're creating now. Every moment is a blank page that we may fill with our choices, actions, and dreams.

December 13th

"To find yourself, think for yourself." – Socrates

When you think for yourself, you empower yourself to build your own future and live your own life. Accept your uniqueness, trust your intuition, and allow your inner wisdom to guide you on the path to self-realization.

December 14th

"The essence of philosophy is that a man should so live that his happiness shall depend as little as possible on external things."
– Epictetus

Our inner peace and joy should be based on our own thoughts, decisions, and ideals. By mastering this concept, we become resilient and well equipped to deal with the ups and downs of life. We learn to enjoy the small things in life and to be content with ourselves.

December 15th

"It is not the strongest of the species that survive, nor the most intelligent, but the one most responsive to change." – Charles Darwin

Accepting change with an open mind and a positive attitude can result in tremendous growth and opportunity. So, let us continue to be open to new ideas, see challenges as chances for progress, and be the ones who thrive in the face of change.

December 16th

"I knew that if I failed I wouldn't regret that, but I knew the one thing I might regret is not trying." – Jeff Bezos

Regret is often the result of wasted opportunities, of allowing fear to hold us back. But you will take a different road, one of bravery and resilience. Accept every opportunity with the idea that your biggest regret would be to not try. Keep that brave spirit alive, and keep pursuing your dreams with a firm belief in yourself.

December 17th

"Happiness is not the absence of problems; it's the ability to deal with them." – Steve Maraboli

Because difficulties and obstacles are a normal part of the human experience, happiness does not imply enjoying a problem-free life. It is instead a matter of mindset and how you choose to respond to those problems.

December 18th

"Whatever we believe about ourselves and our ability comes true for us." – Susan L. Taylor

Believe in yourself, cultivate your self-confidence, and trust that you have what it takes to overcome obstacles and achieve your goals. Your beliefs may be the driving force behind your achievements. Be aware that your mind is a powerful instrument, and with the appropriate mindset, you can accomplish remarkable things.

December 19th

"First say to yourself what would you be; and then do what you need to do." – Epictetus

When you determine who you desire to be, you lay the groundwork for your behaviors to follow. Begin by visualizing the person you wish to become, then make clear goals and take consistent steps toward those goals. Your actions will define your identity, and with persistence and hard work, you'll discover yourself becoming the person you've always wanted to be.

December 20th

"The most important investment you can make is in yourself."
– Warren Buffett

Investing in yourself is like sowing the seeds of your own progress and success. Whether it's through education, personal growth, or pursuing your passions, every effort you make to better yourself is an investment that pays the best dividends. Keep in mind that you are your most precious asset. So, continue to invest in your education, health, and personal development. As you grow, you'll discover that the returns on this investment are enormous.

December 21st

"Many of life's failures are people who did not realize how close they were to success when they gave up."– Thomas A. Edison

Your goals may be closer than you realize, and each step you take brings you closer to attaining what you desire. Remember, it's not how many times you fall that matters; it's how many times you get back up and keep going. Perseverance is frequently rewarded with success!

December 22nd

"When anger arises, think of the consequences." – Confucius

By pausing to consider the repercussions, you are regaining control of your emotions. This simple technique will help you avoid rash decisions and respond to difficult situations with better insight and calm.

December 23rd

"Rules for happiness: something to do, someone to love, something to hope for." – Immanuel Kant

Something to do: Taking part in meaningful activities not only keeps our thoughts engaged, but also provides us with a sense of purpose and accomplishment. Someone to love: Love is a strong force that can provide great joy. Nurturing connections and sharing affection can provide warmth and significance to our lives. Something to hope for: Having dreams and goals, no matter how big or small, offers us a reason to wake up each day with optimism and excitement for the future.

December 24th

"Don't be afraid of your fears. They're not there to scare you. They're there to let you know that something is worth it." – C. JoyBell C.

Fears can be potent indicators of what is genuinely important to you. Accept your fears as possibilities for growth and transformation, and you'll discover that they can lead you to experiences and accomplishments you never imagined.

December 25th

"Compare yourself to who you were yesterday, not to who someone else is today." – Jordan Peterson

Comparing yourself to others can be discouraging and ineffective. Instead, concentrate on your own advancement and development. Every day, aim to be a better version of yourself than the day before. This mindset not only encourages ongoing growth, but it also increases self-esteem and happiness.

December 26th

"The purpose of our lives is to be happy." – Dalai Lama

Our lives should be defined by more than the chase of wealth, achievement, or societal approval. It's about pursuing passions, cultivating relationships, and embracing life's simple pleasures.

December 27th

"A mistake repeated more than once is a decision." – Paulo Coelho

Mistakes are an unavoidable aspect of the human experience, but their significance is determined by how we respond to them. When we make a mistake, we have an opportunity to pause, reflect, and correct our course. However, if we commit the same mistake repeatedly, it changes from an accident to a deliberate choice. This quote emphasizes the importance of self-awareness and accountability.

December 28th

"Reflect upon your present blessings – of which every man has many – not on your past misfortunes, of which all men have some."
– Charles Dickens

We all face challenges, setbacks, and difficulties. These occurrences can be unpleasant and leave long-lasting scars. It's normal to reflect on them, learn from them, and use them as stepping stones for personal development. Fixating on past hardships, on the other hand, can lead to a cycle of negativity, self-pity, and even depression. Instead of concentrating on what went wrong, focus on the now. This isn't about dismissing or denying our past; it's about acknowledging that, despite life's difficulties, there are always reasons to be grateful.

December 29th

"It takes courage to choose hope over fear." – Mark Zuckerberg

Fear is a natural human response that is typically triggered by the unknown or the possibility of failure. It can be paralyzing, preventing us from following our aspirations and fully living our lives. However, when we gather the strength to choose hope, we break free from the chains of fear.

December 30th

"When something is important enough, you do it even if the odds are not in your favor." – Elon Musk

The magnitude of the task should not distract you from focusing on its significance. When something is important to you, when it is aligned with your values and purpose, you will gather the determination and resourcefulness required to overcome the difficulties.

December 31st

"Youth is happy because it has the ability to see beauty. Anyone who keeps the ability to see beauty never grows old." – Franz Kafka

There is an opportunity to discover something beautiful every day, whether in nature, art, human interactions, or even in the little things in life. We embrace a mindset that keeps us ever-young in spirit when we intentionally choose to see and appreciate the beauty in our lives. Our perspective and enjoyment of the beauty around us define our happiness and youth, not our age. Keep your eyes open!